Praise for *Brand You*

'The definitive guide on how to build and grow the most precious brand you'll ever work on: yourself.'

Sir Mark Thompson, Chairman of the Board of Directors of Ancestry; Chief Executive Officer of the Cable News Network (CNN); former President and CEO of *The New York Times* Company and former Director-General, BBC

'A timely reminder that personal branding today is about the real you – your purpose, values and drivers – not some packaged goods strategy. You have to dare to be real. And learn to be self-aware. Ready?'

Avivah Wittenberg-Cox, CEO, 20-First; Speaker and Author

'Personal branding is becoming an increasingly important element that all of us need to consider in today's disruptive world. It can be the differentiator that enables us to show not only our visibility and our talents, but also our personal values. In *Brand You,* David and Sylvana offer a pragmatic and effective roadmap to help everyone become more aware of what developing your personal brand can do for you and what you need to do to make it happen. It's very readable and is highly recommended; to start developing your 'Brand You' today!'

Dave Millner, Founder and Consulting Partner, HR Curator Ltd

'*Brand You* helps to join the dots between who you are and what you do . . . essential reading to help you find your purpose in your career.'

Jo Minns, former HR Director at Coutts; Executive Coach and Consultant

Brand You

Pearson

At Pearson, we have a simple mission: to help people make more of their lives through learning.

We combine innovative learning technology with trusted content and educational expertise to provide engaging and effective learning experiences that serve people wherever and whenever they are learning.

From classroom to boardroom, our curriculum materials, digital learning tools and testing programmes help to educate millions of people worldwide – more than any other private enterprise.

Every day our work helps learning flourish, and wherever learning flourishes, so do people.

To learn more, please visit us at **www.pearson.com**

Brand You

Stand out from the crowd with authentic personal branding

David Royston-Lee
and
Sylvana Storey

Harlow, England • London • New York • Boston • San Francisco • Toronto • Sydney
Dubai • Singapore • Hong Kong • Tokyo • Seoul • Taipei • New Delhi
Cape Town • São Paulo • Mexico City • Madrid • Amsterdam • Munich • Paris • Milan

PEARSON EDUCATION LIMITED
KAO Two
KAO Park
Harlow CM17 9NA
United Kingdom
Tel: +44 (0)1279 623623
Web: www.pearson.com

First edition published 2009
Second edition published 2012 (print and electronic)
Third edition published 2023 (print and electronic)

ISBN: 978-1-292-45728-4 (print)
            978-1-292-72558-1 (ePub)

British Library Cataloguing-in-Publication Data
A catalogue record for the print edition is available from the British Library

Library of Congress Cataloging-in-Publication Data
Names: Royston-Lee, David, author. | Storey, Sylvana, author.
Title: Brand you : stand out from the crowd with authentic personal
    branding / David Royston-Lee and Sylvana Storey.
Description: Third edition. | Harlow, England ; New York : Pearson, 2023. |
    Includes bibliographical references and index.
Identifiers: LCCN 2023035853 | ISBN 9781292457284 (hardback) | ISBN
    9781292725581 (epub)
Subjects: LCSH: Career development. | Business networks. | Branding
    (Marketing) | Success in business.
Classification: LCC HF5381 .P87 2024 | DDC 650.1--dc23/eng/20230831
LC record available at https://lccn.loc.gov/2023035853

10 9 8 7 6 5 4 3 2 1
27 26 25 24 23

This book draws on the previous edition of *Brand You* by John Purkiss and David Royston-Lee, published by Pearson in 2012.

Cover design by Two Associates
Cover image © 300_librarians/iStock/Getty Images

Print edition typeset in 10/14 Charter ITC Pro by Straive
Printed by Ashford Colour Press Ltd, Gosport
NOTE THAT ANY PAGE CROSS REFERENCES REFER TO THE PRINT EDITION

Contents

Contents

Pearson's Commitment to Diversity, Equity and Inclusion

Pearson is dedicated to creating bias-free content that reflects the diversity, depth and breadth of all learners' lived experiences. We embrace the many dimensions of diversity including, but not limited to, race, ethnicity, gender, sex, sexual orientation, socioeconomic status, ability, age and religious or political beliefs.

Education is a powerful force for equity and change in our world. It has the potential to deliver opportunities that improve lives and enable economic mobility. As we work with authors to create content for every product and service, we acknowledge our responsibility to demonstrate inclusivity and incorporate diverse scholarship so that everyone can achieve their potential through learning. As the world's leading learning company, we have a duty to help drive change and live up to our purpose to help more people create a better life for themselves and to create a better world.

Our ambition is to purposefully contribute to a world where:

- Everyone has an equitable and lifelong opportunity to succeed through learning.
- Our educational products and services are inclusive and represent the rich diversity of learners.
- Our educational content accurately reflects the histories and lived experiences of the learners we serve.
- Our educational content prompts deeper discussions with students and motivates them to expand their own learning and worldview.

We are also committed to providing products that are fully accessible to all learners. As per Pearson's guidelines for accessible educational Web media, we test and retest the capabilities of our products against the highest standards for every release, following the WCAG guidelines in developing new products for copyright year 2022 and beyond.
You can learn more about Pearson's commitment to accessibility at:

https://www.pearson.com/us/accessibility.html

While we work hard to present unbiased, fully accessible content, we want to hear from you about any concerns or needs regarding this Pearson product so that we can investigate and address them.

- Please contact us with concerns about any potential bias at: https://www.pearson.com/report-bias.html

- For accessibility-related issues, such as using assistive technology with Pearson products, alternative text requests, or accessibility documentation, email the Pearson Disability Support team at: disability.support@pearson.com

About the authors

David Royston-Lee is acknowledged as an expert in career management for people of all ages. He has a background in recruitment, in human resources, and latterly as a senior executive coach in leadership working globally with individuals wanting to be the best version of themselves. He has been involved in major change projects as well as developing programmes for individuals who want to reassess who they are and what legacy they want to leave within their world of work.

Sylvana Storey, business psychologist and management consultant, is a highly regarded expert in culture change, leadership and diversity, equity and inclusion, and is the founder and CEO of Global Organizational Integrators. During her 30 years in the field, Sylvana has driven major cultural and behavioural change programmes with companies delivering globally and across sectors.

Authors' acknowledgements

—————

Our collaborators on this third edition of Brand YOU, have offered guidance, provided their expert support and contributed generously.

In particular, John Purkiss, the co-author on the first two editions, who with his Brand You experience, meticulously reviewed this edition and offered insightful comments, which has added great value.

Thank you to colleagues who reviewed our book. Specifically, Alice Cipirski, Jo Minns, Stefan Strauss, Grace Mansah-Owusu and Stephen Broadley. We remain greatly appreciative of the time you took, as well as your constructive observations.

To our agent, Jacq Burns for her continuing guidance and activity behind the scenes.

To Rebecca Youé, our Associate Editor and Eloise Cook, Publisher at Pearson, who encouraged and pushed us to continually reflect on the purpose of this edition.

To all our readers who have read our previous editions and have fed back how the exercises in the book have benefited them, we thank you.

To our partners and family members, as ever, we remain indebted for your unconditional support and mindful contributions alongside us in our journey.

David and Sylvana

Publisher's acknowledgements

Text Credits:

16 Kogan Page: Bailey, S. and Milligan, A. (2022) Myths of Branding, Kogan Page; 18 Simon & Schuster: David Ogilvy, Confessions of an Advertising Manhe, Atheneum.; 23 Jeff Bezos: Quoted by Jeff Bezos; 25 Jonathan Guthrie: Quoted by Jonathan Guthrie; 39 Crystal-Barkley Corporation: Adapted from LifeWord Design, Crystal-Barkley Corporation; 40 John Wiley & Sons, Inc: Bill George, Peter Sims, (2007), True North: Discover Your Authentic Leadership, Jossey-Bass, March 9, 2007; 52 Lao Tsu: Quoted by Lao Tsu; 53-54 Crystal-Barkley Corporation: Adapted from Life\Work Design, Crystal Barkley Corporation. Barkley, N. (1995) Crystal-Barkley Guide to Taking Charge of your Career, Workman Publishing; 69 Joe Luft and Harry Ingham: Luft and Ingham, H (1955) 'The Johari Window, a graphic model of interpersonal awareness' Proceedings of the Western Training Laboratory in Group Development, Los Angeles; 86 David Ogilvy: Quoted by David Ogilvy; 87 McGraw Hill: Margaret Mark and Carol S. Pearson, (2001) The Hero and the Outlaw – Building Extraordinary Brands through the Power of Archetypes, McGraw Hill; 95 Beulah Loise Henry: Quoted by Beulah Loise Henry;

Publisher's acknowledgements

100 Madonna Louise Ciccone: Quoted by Madonna Louise Ciccone; 122 Culture at Work Limited: Carol Wilson, The Grow Model, Culture at Work, Retrieved from https://www.coachingcultureatwork.com/the-grow-model/; 126 Harvard Business School Publishing: The Key to Landing Your Next Job? Storytelling, https://hbr.org/2021/05/the-key-to-landing-your-next-job-storytelling; 126 Rob Biesenbach: Quoted by Rob Biesenbach; 132 José Ortega y Gasset: Quoted by José Ortega y Gasset; 139 Tao Te Ching: Quoted by Tao Te Ching; 140 Deepak Chopra: Quoted by Deepak Chopra; 142 Brilliance Publishing: Seth Godin, (2014) Tribes: We Need You to Lead Us, Brilliance Publishing, 22 April 2014; 148 Jeff Bezos: Quoted by Jeff Bezos; 155-156 Srikumar Rao: Quoted by Srikumar Rao; 184 Carl Gustav Jung: Quoted by Carl Gustav Jung; 187 Cyan Books: Milligan Andy, 2004, Brand it Like Beckham, Cyan Books; 194 Future Resume Ltd: Adapted from Future Resume Ltd. Used by permissions.

Introduction

Since writing this book some 15 years ago society has changed enormously and when we look at 'personal branding' it has become polarised.

As you peddle furiously on the hamster wheel of life, you can continue to sleepwalk through your career. You are splintered into wearing different masks for different situations.

On the one hand, with the facilitation of technology and increased digitisation, the 'cult' of celebrity has grown. Increasingly, there seems to be a distinctive need to be 'someone different to who you are', or what you think others expect you to be. Also there is an increasing reliance on social media to authenticate you.

This can create a state of addiction in which you constantly recreate yourself into what you think others want you to be.

The more you do this, the more you lose your sense of self.

How do you put a stamp on who you really are? What masks are you wearing without understanding why? Our third edition helps you to delve under the masks, to step back and create a blueprint to identify your authentic brand.

This edition addresses how you can cut through these complexities to identify:

- How YOU stand out from the crowd to create your authentic brand

- How YOU allow your inner self, who you are, to shine through the noise of daily life
- How YOU identify and use your talents to create a fulfilling vision for your future.

Our inside-out approach provides you with a framework to build a strong sense of self by understanding your purpose, values and talents. We provide you with multiple tools to access and present your individual brand to the world. This will be your compass to achieving a fulfilling career into the future.

You are no longer in a hamster wheel but in the driving seat of determining your life!

David Royston-Lee and Sylvana Storey

part 1

The relevance of branding to you

This first part of the book deals with developing your brand from an 'internal' focus.

chapter 1

Why develop your brand?

In this chapter, we explain the importance of developing an authentic brand. Looking at your context in the world of work, we explain that the job market is changing and a reliance on simply your present skills and past experience will not be enough to remain employable in the future.

We also talk about how ensuring a flexible approach to the job market is easier if you know your brand and the importance of networking. You need to be constantly developing your brand as the world of work evolves. In future chapters, we will concentrate on the three attributes you need to clarify – namely, your purpose, your values and your talents.

Why exactly do you need to develop your personal brand?

Your brand is the way you stand out from the crowd, through your unique combination of purpose, values and talents.

It is about having a clear understanding of who you are, where your energy comes from, and what you would like to achieve and why you want to achieve it. Your energy comes from aligning purpose, values and talents to create a way of being that suits you.

This clarity also helps you to make decisions in your life that 'fit' you. Even more, it helps people to understand you better and attracts people to you.

Increasingly, in the job market, employers are looking for people to 'solve problems' rather than relying on past experience. They are becoming more concerned with how you operate rather than what you have done. Creativity, and curiosity, is becoming increasingly valuable and, therefore, understanding how you operate what your purpose and passions are makes it easier for you to be visible in a world where employers can use the digital global infrastructure to identify talent anywhere in the world.

No longer is reliance on past skills and experience as important. Knowing the uniqueness of your brand and using it to be visible globally is an imperative in terms of future employment.[1]

Give yourself greater flexibility in your career

Knowing who you are allows you to make the right decisions in your life in terms of why, how and what you do with it.

Knowing who you are also helps you to see all the different options open to you. It helps you identify when you feel you are on the right track, or on a track that makes you feel uncomfortable, and where earlier decisions seem to have imprisoned you to taking only one course of action.

As the world of work becomes less reliant on traditional structures, the less likely you are able to manage your career and the more important your brand becomes. To ensure your marketability, you need to understand both who you are and what you can offer the world for mutual benefit. If you do not know what your brand is, you are much more likely to 'play it safe', limiting your view of the world to your present employer. It is far better to build a track record that fits your purpose and values and uses your talents effectively. It stops you from making snap decisions about that next job simply based on a limited view of what you think you 'should' do. This is the essence of personal brand management.

We find ourselves in an extremely complex global market. For example, as the coronavirus has taught us, face-to-face communication is not required as much as it was; you can work or do business with almost anyone, anywhere. Also, the distinction between employment and self-employment has become blurred. More and more people move back and forth between the two. They train with one firm, join another, lose or change their job, freelance and then move to other sectors. They take time out to study or have children. They move to another country and/or start a business.

While all these changes are occurring, it is important to stay with your brand as it gives you energy and keeps you visible, attracting the people who need your services. With the growth of the internet – and social media in particular – the ways of staying visible have multiplied but it is also awash with others trying to be visible at the same time as you, so clarity around your brand is essential.

Knowing your brand helps you to be more visible.

Instead of pursuing a traditional career where you stayed in one organisation or one discipline, you can now tailor your work to your purpose, values and talents. Where in the past it was about climbing up a set ladder dictated by the organisation in which you worked, now, you are more likely to move laterally and build your career in different ways. That is, you can do several jobs that utilise your talents in a multitude of ways for multiple purposes. For instance, the following examples show how purpose, value and talents combine to direct your brand.

- An IT specialist might use their analytical skills to implement the same software package for various organisations but, knowing their brand, may choose to specialise in the arts world where they realised that their analytical skills and creative talent can combine in an industry where that combination is in short supply.

- A human resources partner might realise what excites them most is to move from an operational role to one that concentrated on restructuring organisations to include more diversity and inclusion and find self-employment the best way to utilise and develop their talents.

- A chief executive might realise that, rather than focus on one organisation and sector, their passion lay in making a difference across a number of companies with a multitude of different needs.

Each time, however, you need to learn from the context you are in and moving into, and not make the mistake of using the same blueprint and the same approach for the next role. You need to keep learning to remain flexible to the needs of your next role to ensure your employability into the future. That learning adds to your knowledge of yourself and helps to develop your own brand. Fundamentally, it is more important to be employable than employed.

Showing this flexibility applies whether you are meeting people face to face, or editing your profile on your website or social media platforms. This book will help you do both.

Enhance your career prospects

Loyalty is less important now than it was in the past. Your employer is not a mother or father who will take care of you in good times and bad. We have to learn, to grow up and make our own way in life. Loyalty is now unlikely to be rewarded with job security. Even blue-chip companies fire people who have spent decades working for them.

If you build a positive personal brand, your employer will probably treat you well, in the hope that you will stay. But they and you will be very much aware that, if you are not learning and building your brand, you will move on to another role that will ensure your employability. Loyalty is a two-way process based on trust, which both employer and employee look for from one another.

While loyalty may have declined, commitment remains essential. If you are employed, the best way to keep your job is to produce first-class work consistently. The same applies, even more so, if you are self-employed. If you are known for excellence, clients will keep coming back to you. So, clarifying your purpose, values and your talents is becoming more important in a world where 'standing out from the crowd', and being visible, is vital for employability.

Develop a portfolio career

Another trend is the growth in portfolio careers. A portfolio career comprises a variety of roles rather than one job at a single organisation. A portfolio career helps you to tailor your skills and activities to roles across different organisations. During the COVID-19 lockdown, many organisations realised that 'getting things done' was better served through using portfolio professionals who were faster and more efficient. It also meant they had access to expert talent from around the world. It also reduced fixed costs and provided greater strategic flexibility. For example, there is a growth in experts in their sectors teaching part-time at universities. We also know a successful investor and company chairman who has built a second career as a professional photographer.

Many more people are energised by variety of work, autonomy and a flexible lifestyle. Others work on projects that show the range of their abilities while they look for a new job to help move out of a particular discipline and show their diverse expertise. Technology has made portfolio careers much easier.

Some companies prefer non-executives who work *full time* in a related field. For example, someone working in retail might sit on the board of a bank that wants to apply retail disciplines to its branch network.

The number of angel investors has also grown significantly across the globe. Technology is the fastest growing sector at present, with a real rise in interest from investors. Some people have a full-time job but invest in a start-up company and sit on the board. Others devote most of their time to a portfolio of directorships.

Make better use of your network

Your network is an important source of new opportunities. The key message to put out to your network is to both show the range of capabilities you are able to provide and how you stand out from the crowd. By presenting a full picture of who you are, your network will help you to realise more opportunities within the world of work. It is through these relationships that you are more likely to find your next role, rather than through hiring firms, for example.

Businesses are increasingly valuing those whose networks are strong as it helps keep you up to date with changing professional standards and trends. This is even true in sectors with plenty of specialist hiring managers, such as finance and accountancy. According to LinkedIn, 85 per cent of jobs are now obtained by networking, both in terms of referrals and getting inside information on organisations you are interested in. It also is a great way to understand the market you are operating in and your marketability and value to that market both now and in the future. Building your brand is extremely helpful in this regard – the more your network understands what you do and how you do it the more they will be able to help you achieve what you want.

Even if you are busy right now, it is worth keeping in touch with your network so that you are aware of opportunities open to you that might appeal to you and to help make sure you are always marketable. It is easy to focus on the organisation that employs you now while neglecting your contacts elsewhere and failing to develop new contacts for the future.

Increase your marketability

In your occupation, it is most likely that you have the skills required. But being good at what you do is not enough – you have to market yourself, clarifying how you work and what extra value you can bring to an organisation. If you produce first-class work, your boss or client will value you. However, they may still pay you below the market rate. If you make sure other people know what you can do, there will be several of them bidding for your services.

Knowing your worth in the job market is important.

Short-term salary increases vs long-term employability

In many countries, people change jobs for more money all the time . . . but you have to be careful you do not end up in areas where short-term increases in salary actually mean that, in the long term, your employability suffers.

Think of a boss or client who rates you highly. What if you knew 10 people like them – or 100? If more people knew about you, more of them would want to hire you. Your earnings would almost certainly rise. For this to happen, you need to understand how to appeal to a much wider audience and include them in your network.

Make it easier to market yourself

Most people realise they need to market themselves. However, marketing does not mean simply sending out your CV to all and sundry. That makes you no different from any other jobseeker, particularly when your CV is not focused on each specific job. There is a difference between *marketing* and *selling*. This is how we define them:

- Marketing is building a trusted relationship with your target audience, finding out their needs and telling them how you could meet those needs. It includes reaching out to new people as well as those you already know.

- Selling is the final stage in the marketing process. It is helping potential customers to make a decision. It is making sure you win a particular job or contract.

Some people try to sell themselves in the wrong way at the wrong time. You have probably heard them blow their own trumpets at meetings and social events. The same thing occurs online. They keep talking about themselves and their businesses in glowing terms. Unsurprisingly, other people 'unfriend' or 'unfollow' them. At the same time, both employers and headhunters receive CVs with long-winded introductions explaining how marvellous the author is. All of this is a big turn-off.

Some people have the opposite problem; they are so terrified of selling themselves that they miss out on exciting opportunities.

The key is knowing *when* to sell yourself. There are times when you are expected to do so. You may be competing for a job or an assignment. It is late in the marketing process and you are already on the shortlist. Your potential employers or clients have invited you to make a presentation. They want to know *why* they should choose *you*.

How do you get on the shortlist? Other people's perceptions of you play a major role. They also determine the amount people will pay for your services. If you meet someone for the first time, it helps a lot if they have heard or read about you. You will already have some credibility on which you can build.

Ideally, people should experience you in three different ways, in different contexts. For example, they might hear about you, read about you and then meet you in person.

They might see you on a YouTube video or on a well-regarded website. They might be connected with you on social media, in which case they could have been reading your posts for months. The more widely you are recognised, the greater will be the demand for your services. The most powerful endorsement is when you are recommended to a potential client or boss by someone they *trust*.

You have been marketing yourself since you were a small child, initiating and developing relationships. The same principles apply in your job or business. Most people prefer to work with those they know and trust. A relationship can last for years – maybe even a lifetime. Every now and then, there will be an opportunity to work together.

Give yourself a competitive advantage

Business people deal with brands – their products, services and companies – every day, but often neglect their *personal* brands.

However, in recent years, top executives' earnings have grown much faster than average, bringing them closer to star performers in sport and the media. Some executives now hire consultants to market them to headhunters and potential employers. There are also public relations firms and advertising agencies that specialise in personal branding.

People also pay 'CV writing experts' who claim to rewrite your CV so that you have a better chance of being called for interviews. The issue with this approach is, very often, when you look at your 'improved' CV, it bears no relation to who you actually are.

A brand is an asset in its own right. Agencies such as Interbrand have developed valuation methods that they apply to brands ranging from Nike to Volkswagen. Increasingly, brands are being included as assets on companies' balance sheets. Likewise, your personal brand is an asset that can take on a life of its own. If you develop it correctly, people will keep thinking and talking about you.

Your brand will bring you customers and revenues even when you are not working. Most of us do not need to be household names. It is enough to be well-known among potential customers, clients, colleagues and suppliers, as well as to journalists and other commentators who follow your sector. Having defined who you are and your target audience, you can work out what you are going to do for them, and how you are going to tell them about it.

Find people who want what you offer

There are two main approaches to marketing, both of which have their uses.

The first is to find out what people want and then develop your product or service that meets their needs. Many successful entrepreneurs are good at this. If their first customer is very demanding, so much the better! Once that customer is happy, the entrepreneur uses them as a reference when selling to others. This works with anything from sandwiches to software. It is the 'pull' approach to marketing.

The second approach is to develop your product or service and then find out who wants it. A famous example is the Post-It Note™, invented by accident in 3M's laboratories. The company's researchers discovered a glue that could be applied to a sheet of paper but would not stick permanently to anything else. Likewise, when the personal computer was invented, it was not obvious that large numbers of people would want one in their office, let alone at home or while they were travelling. However, these products were marketed effectively and became worldwide successes. This is the 'push' approach to marketing.

Something similar happens in advertising agencies. The client has a product or service – which may be new or decades old – and asks the agency to find new ways of marketing it. The agency discovers new uses for the product or variations that make it more attractive to more people. One example is Marmite, a savoury spread made from yeast extract, which traditionally has been sold in a glass jar. It is now available in an upside-down, 'squeezy' format. The brand has also been extended to chilli and truffle flavours – and even marmite crunchy peanut butter! – which have enabled the brand to reach new markets.

Personal marketing has more in common with the second 'push' approach.

The better you know yourself, the better you can market yourself.

This concept of knowing yourself is the premise on which our book is built. We will start by helping you discover your *purpose* (the *why?*); second, discover your *values* – what you believe is important in your life and work (*how* you want to live your life). The third step is to discover your *talents* – so you can focus on what you love to do and do well (the *what*). If you are true to your values and your talents, you will be *authentic*.

By doing this, you will naturally attract people – employers, customers and colleagues – who share your purpose, your values and talents and appreciate what you do best. Whether you are employed or self-employed, they will ask for you.

Once you are clear about who you are and what you stand for, it is easier to find out who wants what you have to offer. Trying to be 'all things to all people' simply makes you disappear – as you will not stand out as being different.

Instead of rushing around in search of your next piece of work, sit back for a while and think about your brand. How can you understand it fully and develop it? The stronger your brand becomes, the more easily you will attract the work you want to do – and the rewards that go with it.

Key takeaways

- -

- You cannot afford to be complacent in terms of how you see yourself in the world of work. That world is changing fast and you need to wake up to keeping fit in order to ride the waves of those changes.

- Employers can now scour the world for the best talent to solve their problems. Are you in a position where you can compete with others with similar skills and experiences?

- You need to develop your brand effectively to ensure your visibility and that means being clear about your Purpose, Values and Talents.

- Networking is crucial so you link with those who can support you, but they have to understand what sets you apart and makes you unique.

Note

1 Deloitte survey (2017) 'Navigating new forms of work'.

chapter 2

How do brands work?

When we think about brands, we tend to think about products. In this chapter, we will explain the difference between product and personal brands and the two ways you build a brand, through identifying your unique selling points and developing your brand identity.

Product brands

Brands in the broadest sense have existed for thousands of years. Empire builders have long understood their importance. One example is the Lion of St Mark, complete with wings and a book, which was the symbol of imperial Venice. It stands on a column between St Mark's Square and the gondolas. Visitors to Bergamo, far away in the foothills of the Alps near Milan, are sometimes surprised to see the Lion of St Mark on the side of the Palazzo della Ragione. From the fifteenth to the eighteenth century, the brand reminded people that they were in the Venetian Empire.

The word *brand* has been used in marketing since the mid-nineteenth century, when large factories began to produce soap and other packaged goods. People were used to buying such items from small producers in their local communities. However, the factory owners wanted their customers to trust a non-local product. When the product was ready for shipment, a red-hot iron was used to 'brand' the factory's logo or insignia into the wooden container. Nowadays, there are many definitions of a brand. One of our favourites is this:

A good brand is a promise kept

As Andy Milligan, a leading brand consultant, put it: 'A brand is a symbol that guarantees a particular experience.'[1]

By marketing a reliable, high-quality product, packaged goods manufacturers attracted millions of customers. Brands such as Kellogg's breakfast cereals gradually became as familiar as local farmers' produce. Manufacturers then learned to incorporate particular *brand values* – intangible characteristics that were important to consumers. Certain packaged foods were homely, for instance; they reminded you of the food your mother used to make. Later on, they incorporated other brand values such as youthfulness, fun and luxury.

Personal brands

In British history, Boudica or Boadicea, the wife of a Celtic King, led an uprising against the Roman Army in AD 61. She has been remembered for her brand as a heroine and a symbol of the struggle for justice and independence.

Much more recently, Richard Branson's famous Virgin brand is associated with his inspirational leadership, and for him being a risk taker, an entrepreneur and daredevil. It is also interesting to note that the Virgin brand is always consistent, even though the organisation continues to evolve and diversify from being a record shop to travel to telecommunications. It is one of very few brands where the individual brand is also the organisational brand.

The key to personal brands is they engender *trust* – even if a brand is a negative one. For example, you probably know someone who is always late for meetings. So, you may see them as unreliable and, in relation to their timekeeping, they cannot be trusted. However, other aspects of their brand can be trusted.

Throughout the book, we will be asking you questions about people brands and how you can create your own truly authentic brand and, hopefully, a positive one.

Brand-building

There are two main approaches to brand-building: unique selling proposition and brand identity.

Developing a unique selling point

The first approach is the *unique selling proposition* (USP), which is a powerful tool for attracting customers. Not every brand has a single feature that makes it unique. However, you can still have a USP based on a *unique combination* of benefits to the customer.

For example, a cleaning fluid might remove both grease and limes-cale; a person could be good at both marketing and finance.

Some people aim to be the cheapest. However, there are several potential problems with this. First, if you only compete on price, you may earn very little. Second, any competitor can copy your USP at short notice – all they have to do is drop *their* price. The third problem is that being cheap will drive some customers away – they will interpret cheapness as a sign of poor quality. Top-quality products are sometimes described as 'reassuringly expensive'.

At this point, it is worth clearing up two sources of confusion regarding the USP. First, we are using the word *unique* in its literal sense. It is derived from the Latin word *unus*, meaning *one*. A product or service cannot be 'very unique': it is either unique or it is not. Second, confusion also arises when people talk about 'USPs' in the plural, listing advantages that competitors also offer, such as great customer service and a one-year guarantee. If several people have similar offerings, it is clearly not unique to anyone. Your USP can either be one characteristic or a unique combination of characteristics. A clear USP makes your brand stand out in people's minds.

Developing brand identity

The second approach to brand-building is *brand identity*. One of its strongest advocates was David Ogilvy, the founder of the Ogilvy advertising agency. He argued that brand identity was paramount. In his book *Confessions of an Advertising Man*, he stated that advertisers should 'build sharply defined personalities for their brand and stick to those personalities year after year.[2] It is the total personality of the brand rather than any trivial product difference which decides its position in the market place.'

Brand personalities develop over time, just like human personalities. Some have a heritage stretching back decades or centuries. Several generations from the same family know and love them. You can see this in luxury goods, banking, sports teams, private clubs, charities, cars, cameras, schools and universities. The key is to ensure that the brand identity remains consistent, while the products evolve and the brand itself grows. As we shall see later, *archetypes* are a valuable tool for managing this process.

Evolving brands to meet changing needs

As society evolves, brands must keep up by also evolving.

Attitudes to nutrition and the environment have changed fast, catching some companies off-guard. For example, McDonalds was simply a company that sold burgers. Over time, their brand has evolved to incorporate much more nutritional and environmentally friendly offerings such as fish, salads, children's meals and paper straws.

In the business world, the switch from print to digital has left some businesses behind. During any period of change, the winners remain true to their *values*: deeply held beliefs that they communicate continuously. Their values enable them to retain existing customers and attract new ones.

Key takeaways

- It is just as important to build a personal brand as it is to build a brand for a product.
- For both, 'a brand is a promise kept'. Trust is an important factor, so a brand needs to be authentic.
- Your unique selling point is one unique characteristic or a unique combination of characteristics that help you stand out in people's minds.
- Developing a consistent brand identity is crucial so that it remains while the brand also evolves over time.

Notes

1 Bailey, S. and Milligan, A. (2022) *Myths of Branding*, Kogan Page.
2 Ogilvy, D. (2011) *Confessions of an Advertising Man*, Southbank Publishing.

part 2

Creating your personal brand

Part 2 is where you look at the unique brand you have developed in relation to the external world of work that is of specific interest to you.

chapter 3

Your personal brand

As Jeff Bezos, the founder of Amazon, said, 'Your brand is what people say about you when you are not in the room.'

What if someone you know described you to someone you had never met? What would they say? They might talk about the kind of work you do. For example: 'You are an innovator. You look at things differently.' Or, they might talk about your personality. For example: 'You're always optimistic.' They will remember things about you that stand out for them, your unique way of operating in different situations.

We will show you how to turn your brand into a valuable asset – perhaps your most valuable asset. As with any other brand, your personal brand is based on people's expectations of how you will behave or perform in particular circumstances. The stronger your brand, the more confidence others will have in you. Your brand is a promise kept. It can be communicated through symbols such as your name, your physical appearance or the way you work or live your life.

Your brand needs both reputation and reach

You may have a good *reputation*, but that is not the same thing as your brand. The Latin root of the word reputation is *reputare* – to think repeatedly. There may already be five people who think about you often and ask you to work with them now and then. However, what if 50 or 500 people kept thinking about you? How much busier and wealthier would you be? The greater the number of people who think about you, the greater is your *reach*.

The more often someone thinks of you, and the higher their opinion of you, the stronger your reputation becomes. The larger the number of people who think about you, the greater your reach becomes. In order to build a strong brand, you need both reach and reputation.

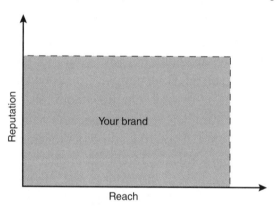

Your brand needs to be actively managed

Your brand is not static, it is constantly developing. If you are employed, your brand affects your visibility and your job prospects. It also determines the number and quality of job offers you receive internally or from other employers. If you are running a business, your brand will help you win customers. Whoever you are, your brand needs to be relevant to the people who are your audience.

Most people have weak brands. When you come back from a conference with a handful of connections, it is hard to remember who was who, let alone what they did or how you might be able to work with them. As Jonathan Guthrie of the *Financial Times* once said: 'Did he import china from Turkey, or turkeys from China?'

If you want to be successful, you must stand out from the crowd. People should remember who you are, what you do and what makes you different. The stronger your brand, the more people will value you. They will be pleased that *you* are working on their project and may pay extra for that feeling of reassurance. Anyone can build a strong brand, from electricians, disc jockeys, plumbers, cleaners, psychotherapists, lecturers to portrait painters.

The professional services sector, including consultants, lawyers and accountants, has grown rapidly. Some professionals spend many years with the same firm, but the issue of personal branding still arises. If you are a junior member of staff, it helps to be well-regarded by several partners, since they will decide who works on each project. They may also support your election to the partnership. Once you become a partner, you suddenly find yourself in a sales role, required to win a certain amount of business. Your personal brand is now more important than ever. Some partners rely heavily on their firm's brand, which can help to ensure they are invited to pitch for new projects. However, it is better to build your personal brand too, so clients ask specifically for you, wherever you happen to be working.

Your brand should be authentic and consistent

A powerful brand has to be *authentic:* based on who you are and what your life and work are all about. You should aim to be the 'best *you*'. Some people project an image that does not fit reality, often by imitating a person they admire or by attempting to conform. The result is artificial and unconvincing. They are sometimes described as *cardboard cut-outs*.

As we said in Chapter 1, the key to building your brand is to know yourself. The first step is to identify your *purpose* – why you do what you do and then link it with the *talents* you were born with. It is best to develop them in a distinctive way, in accordance with your *values*. If you are authentic, people will know what you do and what you stand for. Some people will keep away from you, others will be attracted to you. If you make it easy for people to see what you do and how you do it, their perception will be aligned with reality. If you then extend your brand into a new area, it will make sense to them; they will feel comfortable working with you in a different situation.

You may wish to keep your work and private lives separate. However, it is still a good idea to be consistent. You do not have to tell everyone about your private life, but it helps if what you say in private does not clash with what you say at work or in public. This is particularly important on social networking sites. There are countless examples of people losing their jobs after saying something online that their employers do not like. It is best to assume that everything you write on a social networking site is public. At the very least, someone can copy what you have written and paste it anywhere they like.

Self-employed people often have a natural overlap between their work and their social lives. Friends may become customers or colleagues, and vice versa. If so, it is essential to be the same person at work and elsewhere. Your life will then be integrated and harmonious. Instead of wearing different masks, you can be yourself in every situation.

The more authentic you are, the more attractive you will be to some people and the less attractive you will be to others. If you try to please everyone, you will fail to appeal strongly to anyone. Those who are attracted to you will feel they can rely on you to behave in a certain way.

Your brand can become valuable

A strong brand will make you stand out in the eyes of people who want what you have to offer. They will naturally think of you. If your brand appeals to them, they will choose you. They may even pay a premium to work with you. However, if you do not stand out, they will see you as a *commodity*. Having no particular reason to choose you, they will pay you the going rate at best. Top musicians and film stars illustrate this principle. Their fans buy their latest album or watch their latest film because they are in it. They earn far more than other musicians or actors. The extra money they earn is only partly due to their singing or acting ability. Film, television and digital media have given them a global market that has boosted their earnings enormously.

Personal brands can also acquire an influence that goes way beyond money. Mahatma Gandhi, Nelson Mandela and Mother Teresa have all shaped our world by embodying and promoting a set of *values*, as have Che Guevara, Bob Marley and Mao Zedong. Some people behave as though they do not have a brand or, if they do, it is worth nothing to them. Some entrepreneurs treat their investors badly when they raise money for a business, assuming they will do so only once. This can make it difficult, if not impossible, to raise money for a second venture. Other entrepreneurs focus on serving their customers *and* their investors. They develop a following that helps to make their second business even more successful than the first.

Some interview candidates over-promise and under-deliver. They look good on paper. They sound good when you meet them. However, when you investigate their track record, you find they have achieved little for their employers. They often lack authenticity, claiming to have certain values but behaving in an entirely different way. This damages their brand and their job prospects.

Your brand can outlive you

A personal brand can last for decades, even centuries, continuing to promote who you are. Think of Mozart, Elvis Presley, Nina Simone, Albert Camus, Charles Dickens, Jane Austen and Lao Tsu, author of the *Tao Te Ching* over 2500 years ago. William Shakespeare's brand still generates revenues for the Royal Shakespeare Company, the Globe Theatre in London and his hometown of Stratford-upon-Avon. More so, in this digital age, your use of social media can become your legacy. For example, hiring managers can look back at your digital footprint to confirm the consistency of the messages that you have put forward in the past, which reflect who you are now.

Your job title is not your brand

Some people aspire to a certain title, such as partner, director or chief executive, and cling to it once they have it. They assume that this is who they are. However, your title tells people little or nothing about what you do or what you stand for. It does not make you unique. At most, it indicates your position in a hierarchy and, perhaps, the skills you possess.

A former colleague of ours has turned around 10 companies, including some large, well-known ones. Although his current title is chief executive, he views it purely as a tool to do his job. Sometimes, it is an inconvenience. He describes himself as a *turnaround guy*, which is far more meaningful.

Your brand should stand out like a tall building

Imagine your brand is a building under construction – you want it to be distinctive and clearly visible. Think of the Eiffel Tower, the

Empire State Building or the Taj Mahal. As it becomes bigger and taller, more and more people will notice it. They will start to ask what goes on inside.

However, before you build it, you must first prepare the ground. This brings us to the subject of your purpose – why build it at all?

Key takeaways

- Your personal brand is based on people's expectations of how you will behave or perform in particular circumstances.
- The larger the number of people who think about you, the greater your *reputation* and *reach*.
- Whoever you are, your brand needs to be relevant to the people who are your audience.
- You should aim to be the 'best' *you*. The more authentic you are, the more attractive you will be to those who are important to you.
- Personal brands can also acquire an influence that goes way beyond money.
- Your brand can create a long-lasting legacy.
- Your brand is not about your job title but more about what you can do.
- The aim is to build a brand that stands out.

chapter 4

Discovering your personal brand

This chapter begins to set the scene of how you develop your brand. It starts with one fundamental exercise which underpins the later exercises that help you uncover your purpose, your values and your talents.

The first step: your life story

To discover your personal brand, we will start by helping you discover your *purpose* (the *why?*). Second, we will discover your *values* – what you believe is important in your life and work (*how* you want to live your life). The third step is to discover your *talents* – so you can focus on what you love to do and do well (the *what* you are going to develop). If you are true to your values and your talents, you will be *authentic*.

By doing this, you will naturally attract people – employers, customers and colleagues – who share your purpose and your values and appreciate what you do best. Whether you are employed or self-employed, your talents – they will ask for you.

This does not mean that everyone will love you.

Think of your favourite food. Some people love it, others cannot stand it (Marmite/Vegemite comes to mind). The same applies to you.

Once you are clear about who you are and what you stand for, some people will flock to you; others will keep their distance. This makes it easier to find out who wants what you have to offer.

Trying to be 'all things to all people' simply makes you disappear – as you will not stand out as being different.

Instead of rushing around in search of your next role, sit back for a while and think about your brand.

How can you understand it fully and develop it?

The stronger your brand becomes, the more easily you will attract the work you want to do – and the rewards that go with it.

Our 'brand' and sense of 'who we are' is shaped by many factors in both our personal and professional lives.

For most of us, we tend to look at the future without considering the significant experiences and stories from our past in making decisions about what's next.

All the experiences you have combine in a unique way to create the person you are today and how you interact with the world around you.

Those experiences help to create your 'brand' that you and, hopefully, others see.

Before continuing reading this book, a fundamental task is to understand what has been going on in your life to date.

By examining the past, you will have done the preparation necessary to make the exercises in subsequent chapters much easier to both understand and complete. You will be better placed to see how your purpose, values and talents have emerged.

Exercise 1
Your life story

So, the first exercise is to look back on your life from birth until now.

Please do this in the easiest way for you . . . some draw pictures, others fill in a spreadsheet, and others use Post-it Notes™.

It is useful to start by thinking about the highs and lows in your life to date.

What were the key events in your life so far?

Look at your personal life: early childhood, developing friendships, colleagues, what interested you in school, sports and artistic interests, first love, first partner, birth of children, etc.

What were the high points and low points?

Add in people who were important to you from a work perspective and events that happened in that part of your life that you remember also affected you in some way.

If there are 'gaps' in your life history and you have no immediate recollection of what went on, it is useful to start asking people who were around at the time to see if they can remember anything that might help you remember who you were and what you were doing in those initially forgotten periods.

So, now you have some clarity about the highs and lows in your life up until now.

The next thing to do is identify those times in your life that were 'significant' – both good things that happened or things not so pleasant.

What events were significant enough in your life that they took you on a different path, or changed your mind about yourself dramatically? In other words, what significant events made you the person you are today?

- -

This exercise is extremely valuable, as it starts the process of you thinking about 'why' you did things (your motivations at the time) and 'how' you did them (potentially showing the early signs of how you operate now).

It also sets the scene for the three important elements that you need to explore to truly find out 'who am I' and clarify your personal brand.

1 Your purpose

2 Your values

3 Your talents.

The exercises in this book

At this point, we need to say this task of 'completing' exercises is not actually accurate . . . each exercise is 'ongoing' – there is always more you can find out about yourself.

You have, no doubt, reached some conclusions about yourself after 'completing' this exercise on your life story, but depending on who you are, the stage of completion will be different.

The key point is as long as you are confident you 'know enough' about yourself – then it is fine . . . you can always come back and do some more exploration later when you have the need to. Working on the following exercises in this book will refine your thinking about 'who you are'.

We know that we all have different times when we get bored or frustrated when working on exercises – the 'good enough for now' approach, with all the exercises to come, is the right attitude to have.

Developing rather than building your brand

As you go through subsequent exercises to understand and clarify your purpose, values and talents, you will learn that you are 'developing' your understanding through them. We use the metaphor of a building throughout this book to create a visual you can relate to and, also, often people talk about 'building a brand' like a building.

However, when we think of 'building', it tends to mean there was nothing there in the first place. This is not so for three reasons:

- First, the life story will show how far your brand has already developed through pinpointing the significant milestones in your life.

- Second, there is an assumption in 'building' that there is an end point, when it is finished. This is not so. Like a building, our brand can evolve and be reimagined.

- Third, if you try to build your brand from a blank sheet of paper, rather than analysing and accepting who you are, there is a danger that you may believe you need to be someone different from who you are and you will not be authentic.

This does not mean your personal brand cannot change – you will constantly be developing it and finding more about yourself – it will evolve over time, just like a building, which, as an example, may have been built as a factory initially, then became an events venue and subsequently developed into apartments.

Even when a building is finished, there are always things that will need doing to it as time moves on; rooms will be used for differing purposes, extensions will be added to it, etc. So, do not feel, when working on each exercise in this book, that they need to be 'complete' – they do not!

It is an ongoing journey. Hopefully, you will have some 'eureka' moments along the journey, and you will be much more aware of yourself, your needs and your motivations. It will also give you a structure to understand yourself better and give you more control on what you do and how you do it.

This first exercise is the start of the journey – as you revisit your life to date, you will also see *values* emerging and *talents* being used in different ways because of the influence of your *purpose*.

So, start the journey in the realisation that your life story continues after the point that you have done these exercises. Don't get frustrated that there is no end point; simply move on to other exercises and use the same approach with them.

This will be hard as we are all conditioned to 'finish' tasks.

In this case, we are asking you not to, as the approach we ask you to take will give you much more awareness of yourself in the end.

Key takeaways

- The first step in discovering your brand is to look at your past, look at your context, and what was meaningful in your life in terms of both the high points and low points that have influenced who you are now.

- The life story gives clues to the 'why' and 'how' you operate now, and it underpins the following exercises in this book.

- Address the exercises in this book in terms of doing 'enough' on them rather than trying to 'complete' them – your life is ongoing, and will evolve depending on your circumstances and the context within which you are operating.

- You are not building your brand, you are instead developing it. You are who you are, and 'building' can give the false assumption that you should be something you are not, which may cause you difficulties in the future.

chapter 5

Your purpose

In this chapter, you will clarify your purpose.

This is something that is not taught in school and therefore can feel like a very alien concept. However, your purpose is residing within you, and you just have to make the effort to explore that aspect of yourself; looking at your life stories may have given you some clues already. The information and exercises in this chapter will also help. Aristotle believed everyone and everything has a purpose. For human beings, it is something we *desire* for the sake of itself and not anything else.

Nietzsche believed we fundamentally need to 'become who we are' and that we have a deep desire to find purpose in our lives.

Purpose then:

- is about realising what is right for you to do in your life based on what you see is important and worthwhile

- creates and provides a degree of certainty and confidence in ourselves while, at the same time, allowing adaptability to changing circumstances as we go through the journey of our lives.

Therefore, this is the fundamental bedrock of our existence – it answers the question *why* do I exist . . . what for?

It encompasses exploration of new paths that you find exciting and stimulating, doing something you believe is worthwhile and helpful to you, your family, community and society at large.

Purpose is about knowing what risks you choose to take, rather than being directed by others. It is about being consistent in following a path even in the face of dissent or adversity – living your life for yourself not others.

> '**Without purpose life holds little meaning apart from competing with others or keeping up with what is socially acceptable.**
>
> **Without purpose motivation is hard to achieve and passion is just a word.**
>
> **Without purpose learning is a chore, as nothing may interest you.**
>
> **Without purpose you reduce the chances of living a fulfilled and satisfying life.'**
>
> **lifehack.org**

Purpose as the foundation

The idea that each of us has a purpose is new to many people and is often confused with goals or objectives. This diagram will help to clarify the subject.

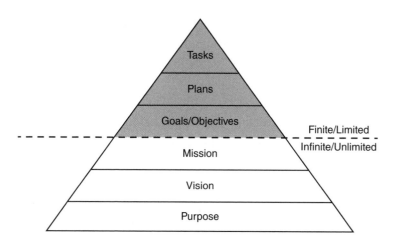

The path from purpose to task

Source: Adapted from LifeWord Design, Crystal-Barkley Corporation.

Often, purpose, vision, mission, goals, objectives, plans and tasks are used interchangeably but this is wrong.

The simplest way to understand and differentiate between them is:

- *Purpose:* describes *why* we exist and the impact we want to make – it is aspirational,
  e.g. 'to serve others'. At this point, there is no picture in your head.
- *Vision*: *what* fulfilling our purpose will look like at some time in the future – it is inspirational,
  e.g. 'knowing I am giving others what they need'. With vision a picture emerges.
- *Mission*: describes what we do and *how* we plan to do it,
  e.g. 'supporting my family and colleagues to be the best they can be'. This is how you begin to 'fill in' the picture.
- *Goals*: long=term undefined, intangible, achievable outcomes – where you want to go,
  e.g. becoming a learning and development director.

- *Objectives*: short-term definable, tangible and measurable outcomes – to get to where you want to go, e.g. getting a qualification that supports your goal towards becoming a director.

- *Plans*: are about what you are going to do to achieve the objectives, e.g. researching the courses available.

- *Tasks*: immediate action to achieve objectives, e.g. identifying the course that bests suits your need and applying.

Goals/objectives, plans and tasks are *finite*. Sooner or later, you can complete a task, carry out a plan or achieve a goal. These are fleeting as you complete them. Your purpose, vision and your mission, however, are *infinite. These remain with you and are never fully completable – they draw you on and evolve as you continue to grow and learn.*

Your purpose ranks above all else. It is the direction that is right for you. Your purpose underpins your values and your talents. Your purpose underpins your life. It can be the reason why you connect with some people and not others, as part of something bigger than ourselves. Psychologists believe this can help create a more meaningful and satisfying life.[1]

Bill George, professor at Harvard, says that just as a compass points towards a magnetic field, the 'True North' of your internal compass pulls you towards your purpose.

He says:

'Although others may guide and influence you, your truth is derived from your life story, and only you can determine what it should be – that's where you come from, and being true to your life story, accepting who you are is one of the hardest things to do.'

Bill George, *True North – Discover Your Authentic Leadership*[2]

You know you are pursuing your purpose when your whole being seems to resonate with what you are doing. You may feel a rush of energy and enthusiasm when you are *active* in a particular situation, however fleeting it may be.

This is often termed as being in 'flow' from the work of Professor Mihaly Csikszentmihalyi, Professor of Psychology.[3] This has been utilised by other books such as *The Rise of Superman* by Steven Kotler,[4] where he proved this concept to be useful when working with extreme athletes to enhance their performance. Subsequently, in a 10-year study by McKinsey,[5] top executives were shown to be 5 times more productive when they were in 'flow'.

So, how do you start to find your purpose?

Exercise 2
Finding your purpose
- -

First, give yourself some space to reflect on your life; find a place where you feel comfortable and are away from distractions.

Have a notepad by your side and first think, 'What is my purpose?'

- What is important to me?
- What gives me energy?
- When do I lose track of time because I'm so engrossed in what I'm doing?

Do not over-think or force the answers; let your mind wander and write down whatever comes into it.

If nothing comes to mind, change tack and ask yourself:

- What would having clarity about my purpose look like in my life?
- How would I be different?
- What would I be doing?

- -

Do not fall into the trap that many people believe is the right way to go about this and not think of yourself first. Often, writers on the subject suggest it is about being 'selfless', thinking about others. Actually, it is about being in a position of 'selfness' somewhere between selfless and selfish.

As in so many cases, it is best to help yourself first before helping others.

This does not mean helping others is not part of your purpose, it always is, but there needs to be a recognition of why you are doing it for yourself first, e.g. when you board a plane, the safety instructions are for you to put the oxygen mask on yourself first, before helping others.

Discovering what you can't stop doing

You can gain valuable insights into your purpose by looking at the things you cannot stop doing. When you are immersed in these activities, you are likely to lose track of time. This experience has been given many names. Athletes, as discussed above, often call it 'being in the zone' or being 'in flow'. You do not think about what you are doing, you just do it. For example, someone we know often loses track of time when she is looking for simple solutions to complex problems. On one occasion, someone told her a problem could not be solved so she started working on it when she got home. When she finally stopped for a cup of coffee, she realised it was 4 am!

Similarly, the 'turnaround guy' we mentioned in Chapter 3 cannot resist reviving a business in distress. This is based on his underlying values, which include hard work, never giving up and acting with a strong social conscience. The talents he applies include analysis, planning, negotiating and persuading people to take action. Every organisation he deals with has a unique set of problems, so he is always developing and improving his skills.

Exercise 3
What you can't stop doing

- -

A good way to look at this may be to reverse the process and ask others first what they see in you. If you ask other people how they perceive you, they may say you have a passion for something that is more obvious to them than it is to you. Ask your friends and/or family to tell you about the things you cannot stop doing. Jot down what they have said and look at expanding on it from your own perceptions. Does the feedback resonate with you? Does it make you think of related things you can't stop doing that they did not see? Make a list of all the things you keep doing, whether or not anyone pays you to do them. Include any activity, whether you have labelled it as work, fun, a hobby, a distraction, or anything else.

. . . .

. . . .

. . . .

. . . .

. . . .

. . . .

. . . .

- -

Once you have your list of things you cannot stop doing, you can begin to identify the themes that connect them.

When you stand back from the last exercise, are there any themes emerging or links?

Exercise 4
Themes that underlie what you can't stop doing

- -

When you look at your list in the previous exercise, can you group your answers in any way?

Are there any activities that are similar in different things that you can't stop doing?

Are there strong values that underpin the things you can't stop doing?

Are there particular talents that you need to use?

Jot down any ideas that come to mind:

. . . .
. . . .
. . . .
. . . .
. . . .
. . . .
. . . .

- -

As you can see, already there is recognition that your values and your talents work with your purpose to make you the person you are.

Personal purpose statement

Once you have identified the themes, you can start to think about putting together your personal purpose statement (PPS).

This statement defines who you are and the mark you want to make on the world . . . the mark is your personal brand.

This statement should be reasonably short and memorable; it will probably not be perfect at this stage. Next, we will look at exercises to define your values and talents more clearly, which may, when you look back on your statement, alter its focus . It is important that we check the result of all the exercises with each other to make sure we are satisfied they are in sync.

It should be written in the present tense so that you can see that it resonates with you *now*.

Do not overthink it – this can lead to paralysis of your thinking and feeling – going back to the term 'selfness', your statement should come from a balance of thinking and feeling.

And remember, purpose is not what you want to do, it is something life calls out of you to do. You might not know it immediately and certainly it is not just about being happy.

The life-story exercise helps enormously in checking your statement as it is a summary of that 'life story' that Bill George referred to earlier.

The important thing to note here is for some finding their purpose is easy, others find it triggered by positive or negative events in their lives. For the majority of people, they need to search for it – and it takes time.

Exercise 5
Personal purpose statement (PPS)

- -

Write down your first attempt at a succinct PPS.

Here are some PPS examples that might help you in doing this:

- To play a significant role in creating a company culture where all workers feel appreciated, so that they feel like their time with the company is a worthwhile investment in themselves, their families and their future.

- To create communication devices that free individuals up to spend more quality, in-person time with loved ones. I want to make devices that foster more work–life balance.

- To empower marginalised young men by giving them the resources they need to overcome racial, educational, political and socioeconomic barriers and injustices.[6]

- -

Pursuing your purpose

Once you are clear about your purpose, your work will be much more meaningful and satisfying. You will have a strong sense of who you are. This will enable you to build a powerful brand and be much more successful. Then you can work on your vision, mission and goals that fit your purpose.

Unfortunately, a lot of people skip these first steps.

Please don't!

It is not just about pursuing goals that provide instant gratification. There should be a reason that lies beyond what you are doing, whether it be a qualification, or job, or material possession or retirement.

The usual reaction is to set another goal, and another, and another. You may be busy planning and taking action, but the satisfaction from achieving goals in isolation is shortlived. It is like being a hamster on a wheel: running hard to achieve a sales target, to save a sum of money or to lose a certain amount of weight. Setting and achieving arbitrary goals does not answer the question: *Why?* Why are you doing what you do? If you do not know, you may wake up one day and realise that your life is meaningless.

Pursuing endless goals can lead to problems. For example, there are many sportspeople who become unhappy once their physical abilities decline. Many successful business people die shortly after retirement. We will come back to the subject of goals below.

Pursuing your purpose could mean that you follow a recognised career path. Equally, you might do things that make more sense to you than they do to other people – at least for the time being. George Orwell, the author and essayist, experienced many facets of life that enriched his writing. Following his education at Eton College, he worked in Myanmar, lived among the homeless, worked at the BBC in London and fought in the Spanish Civil War. These influences are evident in his writing, including *Down and Out in Paris and London*, *Animal Farm* and *Nineteen Eighty-Four*.

Katherine Johnson, an African-American space scientist and mathematician, is a leading figure in American space history and has made enormous contributions to America's aeronautics and space programs by her incorporation of computing tools. She played a huge role in calculating key trajectories in the Space Race – calculating the trajectory for Alan Shepard, the first American in space, as well as for the 1969 Apollo 11 flight to the moon. Johnson is well known for her attention to detail, particularly when it came to the safety of those going into space. She is now retired and continues to encourage students to pursue careers in science and technology fields.

Jobs, businesses, books, etc. are *vehicles* for pursuing your purpose. For example, Deepak Chopra is an endocrinologist who no longer treats patients individually. He has written dozens of books on mind/body medicine and spiritual topics and speaks to audiences all over the world. Another example is Albert Schweitzer, who was, among other things, a doctor and a gifted musician. He used the proceeds from his recitals of Bach's organ works to finance a hospital in French Equatorial Africa. He wrote several books and was awarded the Nobel Peace Prize.

Top athletes train hard for years in pursuit of their goals, such as being the best at what they do. Once they retire, it is important for them to pursue their purpose in other ways, one of which might be to act as a role model for young athletes and support them in fulfilling their potential. In the UK, Tanni Grey-Thompson was a Paralympic wheelchair champion, winning 11 Gold medals until she retired. Now Baroness Grey-Thompson is well-known as a politician and television presenter and considered one of the most powerful women in the UK.

People with a clear sense of purpose often find several ways to express it. Many of them never retire. They continue to pursue their purpose, moving from one way of expressing it to another. Doing what they love gives them energy. They may even say they are putting their heart and soul into their work. Some people carry on working long after they have enough money to last a lifetime. Pablo Picasso once said that when he worked, he relaxed. Doing nothing made him tired.

Key takeaways

- -

- Purpose is the fundamental bedrock of our existence, yet it is often ignored.

- Understanding 'The path from purpose to tasks' diagram is useful, so that we are able to clarify the steps between them to gain a deeper understanding of both the intention and direction of our journey.

- Working on a personal purpose statement (PPS) is an imperative – without it, there is no rudder to your boat.

- Without purpose, life can easily become meaningless.

Notes

1 Arthur Brief, Organisational Psychologist and Professor Emeritus at Utah University.

2 George, B. with Sim, P. (2007) *True North*, Jossey-Bass.

3 Csikszentmihalyi, M. (2008) *Flow – The Psychology of Optimal Experience*, Harpers.

4 Kotler, S. *The Rise of Superman*, Quercus.

5 'Increasing the "meaning quotient" of work', *Mckinsey Quarterly*, 2013.

6 From Happierhuman.com

chapter 6

Understanding your vision and mission

Once you understand your purpose, you can clarify your vision, the *what* you want to do, and your mission, the *how*.

Clarifying both enables you to create a picture in your head of both what you want to do and how you might go about it.

Vision provides the helicopter view of how our brand can better serve others. Defining your mission will move you closer to how you can achieve this.

This chapter will show you how to define your brand by articulating both your vision and mission, which moves you from the intangible towards the tangible.

Vision statement

A vision statement is a future-focused short statement. It is aspirational, explaining where you want to go, or what you hope to achieve in the future. In your mind's eye, it would be like a path leading somewhere. It links directly with your purpose, but it doesn't explain how you are going to get on to that path.

Exercise 6
Your own vision statement

- -

Try creating a vision statement based on the PPS you worked on in the previous chapter.

Is the vision statement inspirational for you?

Does the potential journey fill you with a degree of excitement?

How will you know as you move along your life journey that you are on the right track?

An example might be: 'To affect people's lives positively around the world.'

- -

Having a clear vision creates more energy for the things you love to do and therefore makes life much more meaningful. You will be on your way to fulfilling your potential if you can begin to see how your brand can make a difference and what impact it has on both you and others.

Mission statement

The mission statement is different from a vision statement as it goes into the *how* you will achieve it. It gives a stronger sense of where you are going and provides the direction for finite tangible goals to be created. It also acts as a guiding statement to frame all of your strategic decisions. Your mission statement communicates to outsiders who you are and how you operate differently from others.

Exercise 7
Your own mission statement

- -

Try creating a mission statement based on the PPS and your vision statement.

Does your mission statement explain how you might reach your vision?

Does the way you have written it convey how you work?

Is it an authentic representation of what you are capable of doing that adds value to others?

If we use the previous example vision statement 'To affect people's lives positively around the world', then your mission might be to:

- feed starving people by working as a biochemist, exploring ways to produce new strains of seed that flourish in difficult environmental conditions

- work in finance to help gain access to funding to build better lives for their communities.

- -

Ensuring that your vision and mission statements align with your decisions and activities

If you are facing a decision about a job or business opportunity, ask yourself: 'Does this fit my vision and mission – what I want to do? 'Does this fit how I want to work?' You should get a clear yes or no in reply. If the answer is yes, it is worth investigating the opportunity further. If the answer is no, you can spend your time looking at other opportunities that feed your passion.

You may also have experienced the following situation.

You have succeeded in one role and are considering what to do next; you are presented with an opportunity that uses all your talents but is very similar to your last job. Do you want to go back to that? Is the role sufficiently energising or is it just 'safe'? Will it fire you up? Is it a challenge you cannot resist, or will you just end up achieving more of the same goals? Do you feel trapped by the suggestion that this is all you can do?

If you find yourself in a situation like this, it helps to pay attention to how you *feel*. Does the opportunity resonate with you? Does it feel right for you, or are you simply scared of looking beyond it?

Only you know if a particular job or business is right for you. Sometimes, it is better to leave the question unanswered for a while, so you can avoid making hasty decisions, giving yourself enough time to consider all your options.

As Lao Tsu said: 'To know that you do not know is the best.'

The answer is most likely to come to you when you are relaxed and thinking about nothing in particular. You could be lying in the bath or going for a walk in the park. It helps to be away from crowds, buildings and traffic. Some people find that meditation empties their minds of distracting thoughts and emotions. The way forward suddenly becomes clear. It may be a feeling about what you should do next. Some people describe it as an inner voice, telling them which way to go.

Many people who have explored their purpose, vision and mission find their path in life becomes clearer over time, as they learn more about themselves. Also, by considering different options, you can identify themes that resonate with you. Even what on the surface seems an unsuitable job may open up learning opportunities that can be valuable. It may also show you what you *do not* enjoy or do well at, so you can avoid similar options in the future.

We know a hedge fund manager who was offered an extremely lucrative role in New York. He turned it down in favour of a 12-week cookery course that he had dreamed of doing for some time. He found the cookery course gave him much more energy and he explored ways in which he could use his experience and came to realise that he had come to a point where he needed to try something new and needed an outlet for his creativity. He also realised he wanted to be entrepreneurial and build up a business, without the need to conform to the structure and processes of a large financial institution. He subsequently joined a smaller hedge fund part time, doing what he enjoys and does well. He now looks for companies to invest in, particularly those that will fit with his values . . . and his love of cooking.

With a clear sense of purpose, you can set some goals that are aligned with the vision and mission you have in your head and heart. You can also formulate goals and plans and make a list of the tasks that you will need to carry out.

Establishing goals

Each of your goals will lead you to an action plan. It might include getting up early every day to write another 500 words for your book or running every day to compete in a marathon competition.

Your action plan will consist of a series of tasks. Some of them will be mundane. If you are a doctor, for example, one of your tasks will be to wash or disinfect your hands between patients to avoid spreading germs. However, since this task is aligned with your purpose, vision and mission, it will be both important and meaningful for you.

The following exercise may help you even more to refine both your vision and mission statements and the goals that come out of it.

We have used an example person throughout to help you to think through how you would approach the exercise.

Exercise 8
A thousand times your income
- -

We have some news for you. A distant relative, whom you have never even heard of, has died and left you a thousand times the amount of money you normally earn in a year. However, there is one condition: you have to spend all of it on yourself. You have four minutes to write down exactly how you will spend it.

(Four minutes later.) There is a second instalment to the bequest, for the same amount. However, this time you are not allowed to spend any of it on yourself, only on other people. How will you spend it? You have three minutes to write it all down.

(Three minutes later.) The final clause in the will states that, once you have completed the two steps described above, you will be given unlimited money forever and be granted eternal life. Now that you have unlimited time and money, what will you do? You have two minutes to write it down. Please note that your friends and relatives remain mortal.

Now, go back and read what you have written. What are the themes that emerge? What do they say about you? What is stopping you from doing what you want to do *now?* Are you using money as an excuse for not doing it? What could you do differently from now on? Is there a way of doing what you want without vast sums of money?

When you have worked on the exercises in the following chapters on values and talents, come back to this exercise and ask yourself:

- What are the links between these exercises? There are usually common themes.

- Are there any further clues to refine your purpose?

- What is the *essence* of the work you do best?

- What do you want to do (your vision)?

- How do you want to do it (your mission)?

- What is the first step you need to take (a goal)?

- What also is the *context* in which you do it?

Looking back at what you have written as your purpose statement, does this exercise add anything or focus your statement in any way?

Adapted from LifeWork Design, Crystal Barkley Corporation[1]

- -

An example

This is what someone wrote, identifying points which were linked to their vision, mission and goals:

A distant relative has left you a thousand times the amount of money you normally earn in a year. You have to spend all of it on yourself.

- Learn to fly to travel the world (goal).
- Find a plot of land and design and build a house (goal).
- A private box at a Premier Football Club (goal).
- Holidays around the world, going to all the places I have ever wanted to visit (goal).
- Intensive music lessons on the banjo and the guitar (goal).
- Scuba diving equipment and lessons (goal).

This time you must spend all of the money on other people.

- Set up a children's hospice (vision).
- Set up a fund to give young homeless people a more positive future (vision).
- Give to other charities that help people to learn and apply useful skills, such as computing (mission).
- Make my parents' home easier for them to live in as they get older (goal).
- Give all my relations whatever they need most (goal).
- Give money to my partner to develop their business (goal).
- Get a full-time carer to help my mother look after my father, who has senile dementia (goal).

➤

- Build an extension to my parents' house so we can look after dad better (goal).

- Invest money for the hospice I have supported all my life, to pay for extra counselling for the families and more nursing staff (mission).

- Set up drama courses in my area for young people (vision).

- Give money to charities that I believe in (mission).

You have been granted eternal life and unlimited money. What will you do? Your friends and relatives remain mortal.

We appreciate that you might find this exercise difficult to consider eternal life without the people you love, but try your best:

- Do more to find a partner for the first lifetime – someone with whom I share some common values – *they realised they were looking for perfection in a partner. This exercise helped them realise this, which was really important in their life (goal).*

- Consider becoming an expert in some form of environmental cause (goal).

- Keep abreast of developments that might affect the human race and its survival (mission).

- Decide every 50 years which new subject I can excel in and where in the world I will be based (goal).

- Become an expert guitar and banjo player (goal).

- Develop fundraising skills. Work in every aspect of sales, marketing and fundraising, so I can be even more effective (mission).

- Set up research into degenerative diseases (vision).

- Spend time with innovation centres around the world looking for new ways of solving the world's problems (mission).

- Learn to paint (goal).
- Become an architect (goal).

They then took the list they had created and identified what they considered their vision, mission and goals to help them to explore each.

The vision statements were:

- Set up a children's hospice.
- Set up a fund to give young homeless people a more positive future.
- Set up drama courses in my area for young people.
- Set up research into degenerative diseases.

The mission statements were:

- Give to other charities that help people to learn and apply useful skills, such as computing.
- Invest money for the hospice I have supported all my life, to pay for extra counselling for the families and more nursing staff.
- Give money to charities that I believe in.
- Keep abreast of developments that might affect the human race and its survival.
- Develop fundraising skills. Work in every aspect of sales, marketing and fundraising, so I can be even more effective.
- Spend time with innovation centres around the world looking for new ways of solving the world's problems.

The goal statements were:

- I will apply to the boards of charities that work to campaign on causes that interest me.
- I will enlist in activity holidays that allow me to meet people as well as help me to explore my hobbies further.

- I will consider doing an educational course where the subject matter intersects with both architecture and the environment.

Having looked at their vision and mission statements, they concluded that the ones where they could make an immediate difference focused on 'giving young people a more positive future'.

Given their background in IT, as well as their relationship with a small organisation that provided drama courses, they realised they could capitalise on two avenues. First, they could develop programmes for young people to explore computing. Second, they could connect and introduce them to the drama organisation so that they could develop their confidence and communication skills through drama.

As is often the case, they realised that a lot of the things they wanted for themselves were now within their reach:

The goals were easy:

- They could learn to fly. They might not be able to afford a plane of their own, but they could still qualify as a pilot.

- They could not find a plot of land but were able to renovate an old house by the sea and rent it out.

- They could support their favourite football team, without the private box.

- They could still visit all the places they wanted around the world, whenever there was sufficient money and time . . . and clients close by made it much more possible.

- Intensive music lessons were eminently possible. They decided to investigate and ended up learning the banjo.

- The following year they visited Thailand and went scuba diving for the first time.

They worked with a charity that helps young people build their confidence. They created programmes bringing in relevant people from outside who were experts in communication, computing and confidence building to strengthen the programmes. This enabled them to manage their time with their present organisation and, at the same time, allowed them to spend at least a day a week developing these services for young people.

Looking at the example:

- Can you see the potential links between these exercises?
- Can you see any clues to your own purpose?
- What is the *essence* of the work you do best?
- *How* do you do it?
- What is the *context* in which you do it?

The example person saw several themes in terms of their motivation and relationships. They enjoyed making things run smoothly and had a passion for helping people to fulfil their potential.

They also realised that they did not want to take certain *physical* risks. Learning to fly was more of a dream than something they really wanted to do. It was more about freedom, and that freedom they could see also extended to the young people they were helping – giving them the freedom to grow and develop satisfying lives.

Completing these exercises made their priorities much clearer to them.

They realised that they had been looking for the wrong kind of partner in their personal life. Above all, they needed someone who shared the same things that were important to them, so they could build a harmonious relationship.

They also realised that they liked being the centre of attention, building something that would last. They enjoyed looking after other people in a constructive way. Supporting people for the future came up as a theme in everything they did, from relationships to business.

When they looked back at their purpose, everything they had written down fell into place for them.

Key takeaways

- -

- A vision statement is a future-focused short statement. It is aspirational, explaining *where* you want to go or *what* you hope to achieve in the future.

- A mission statement is different from a vision statement as it goes into the *how* you will achieve it.

- Both help you to clarify who you are, what path you want to follow and how you operate.

Note

1 Barkley, N. (1995) *Crystal-Barkley Guide to Taking Charge of your Career*, Workman Publishing.

chapter 7

Your values

If you look at your brand as a building, your purpose is the reason why you built it, your vision is what it was built for and your mission is how it was built. Your values, in fact, underlie all of them and act as the foundations and, without foundations, the building will be unstable. For most people, their 'values' are below the surface and, when asked about them, they are confused as to what they are and how important they are in determining the shape of their brand.

Knowing your values is important for two fundamental reasons.

First, it helps you make your life easier by realising why you are making decisions or taking actions, as your values dictate how you approach both. Understanding these may mean you are able to make quicker and better choices and also supports our confidence in our sense of self and helps protect our mental health.

Second, it helps others – the clearer they can see your values the easier it is to trust you. We talk about people 'wearing their heart upon their sleeve', meaning that there is no insincerity or pretense – we all know who you are.

In a world of complications and confusion, people who know themselves stand out from others like a beacon, attracting others who can feel safe in their presence.

What are your values?

Your values are *what you believe you stand for*. They are evident in the *way* you do things. Having clarity on what your values are and promoting them is the best way to attract people to you. When other people know your values, they find it easier to trust you, even if they don't agree with you. They know where you stand.

Values can range from a belief in working hard or not keeping others waiting to deeper principles such as putting others first or protecting the environment. There are other values that might be about 'winning at all costs' or 'me first,' which can be seen in either a positive or negative light. The key issue is that you reflect your values in everything you do so others see both consistency and clarity.

Being true to your values also helps you stand out from the crowd. You become like a magnet, attracting people who hold similar values, whether they are friends, customers, colleagues or suppliers.

The first step is to *identify* your values. The second step is to *project* them. The third step is to *check* them. The following exercises will help you with this.

Exercise 9
Identifying your values

- -

Start the process of examining your values by looking back on the first exercise.

Key moments in your life to date, key events that you believe had an effect on who you have become, can be both positive and negative – values come from both.

Ask yourself the following questions:

- What was I doing?
- What underpinned my actions?
- What was driving me?
- Why did I choose the course of action I took at that time?

- -

Our example person had an abusive parent who they avoided as much as they could. However, looking back on what happened, they could see that, through the beatings, instead of believing themselves a victim, they learned courage and resilience, even though this led to more beatings. They stood up to their parent and realised they have carried that value until now in that they do not tolerate any form of coercion or bullying . . . They recognised situations later on in their life where they have stood up to bosses who exhibited those traits. They also realised why they had left companies that were 'based on the survival of the fittest'. It also made them very aware of the other values that evolved from that time in their life – 'risk taking', 'analysis of situations before taking action', etc.

Exercise 10
What you admire in others

- -

Sometimes, it is easier to look to other people and admire something about them rather than begin with yourself. We often project our values on others that we admire while not realising we hold them ourselves.

Write down the names of all the people you admire most, in the space below. Include friends and neighbours, close or distant members of your family, world leaders, authors, artists, sportspeople, media personalities, colleagues, and so on. Include the living and the dead. You can also include fictional characters, from television, film or literature. Write down as many as possible – aim for at least 20.

Name

1 ....

2 ....

3 ....

4 ....

5 ....

6 ....

7 ....

8 ....

9 ....

10 ....

11 ....

12 ....

13 ....

14 ....

15 ....

16 ....

17 ....

18 ....

19 ....

20 ....

21 ....

22 ....

23 ....

24 ....

25 ....

Now for the *second* step.

Take another look at your list above. Next to each name, write down the qualities you admire in that person. Try to give a phrase rather than a noun – so, instead of saying 'confidence', try to explain what is going on behind that word such as 'belief in themselves'. 'Decisive' might be defined as 'making decisions on the basis of what they believe as right, rather than to please others'.

We are interested in what *you* see exhibited in each person (even if you don't know them, it is your perception of what they stand for).

If you see the same quality in a number of the people you admire, you should write it down for each of them.

The *third* step:

Review what you have written and think about the qualities you admire in others. Themes will emerge. You will see a number of qualities repeated in slightly different ways. Which qualities *resonate* most for you? Consider those that appeal to you rationally, emotionally and spiritually.

If there are similar qualities, look at writing a phrase that typifies them all for you.

These *qualities* may reflect your *values*.

For most people, three to five values are enough. After that, there tends to be some overlap so try to stand back from yourself and ask the following questions:

- 'Do the phrases reflect what I stand for?'
- 'If I look at my life story, can I see how these phrases have affected my actions?'
- 'Are these phrases a true reflection of my values – are they unwaveringly me – not just 'nice to have for now' but will guide me throughout my life?
- Do the values underlie my purpose, vision and mission?

In the space below, write down the three to five values that matter most to you:

1 . . . .
2 . . . .
3 . . . .
4 . . . .
5 . . . .

An example

When our example person completed this exercise, they produced the following list of people, with the reasons why they admired them:

1 Muhammad Ali – brilliant at what he did. Used his celebrity status for a cause.

2 Carl Lewis – a great athlete.

3 Bob Geldof – passionate about changing the world.

4 Captain Scott – a courageous adventurer who risked everything.

5 Ellen MacArthur – determined to succeed.

6 My father – amiable, good with people, pragmatic and charming.

7 My mother – witty, intelligent, hard-working, resourceful, with strong morals.

8 Tim (a friend of mine) – intelligent, kind, thoughtful, great at managing teams.

9 Sebastian (another friend) – stoical, thoughtful, energetic, fights for what he believes in.

10 Nelson Mandela – courageous freedom fighter. Fought for his beliefs. Suffered but forgave his captors.

11 Martin Luther King – a courageous civil rights campaigner who died for a cause.

12 Steve Redgrave – committed, with the grit to carry on.

13 Alex Ferguson – a wonderful appetite for success over a long period.

14 Lucian Freud – shocking, provocative art.

15 Jill (a friend) – worked her way up from the bottom to become a successful business person.

16 Kelly Holmes – overcame injury and persevered to reach her goal.

17 Neil Armstrong – a courageous adventurer who risked everything.

18 Aung San Suu Kyi – a courageous campaigner who risked everything for her cause and is now hidden from sight.

19 Terry Waite – imprisoned while promoting peace and understanding.

20 My drama teacher – for giving me confidence.

21 Richard (my ex-boss) – quiet, gets on with it, brilliant mind, confident.

22 George (our former CEO) – engaging, clever, hard-working, strong values.

23 Gerald (ex-colleague) – intelligent, strong self-belief, entrepreneurial.

24 Helen (ex-boss) – genius, financial wizard, multi-talented, charming.

25 Margaret Thatcher – visionary, intelligent, stubborn, insatiable appetite for work.

So, based on this list, our example person identified the following values, in order of importance to them:

1 Courage – determination to keep going, even when faced with hardship

2 Thoughtfulness and kindness to others

3 Risk taking for a cause

4 Robust, intelligent analysis

They realised that they had been expressing these values through the following activities:

1 Working hard to find solutions to complex problems.

2 Developing new ways of working that are more practical and effective.

3 Developing other people's strengths through challenging projects.

4 Recognising the difficulties that could emerge from their actions.

They also mentioned situations and jobs where their values had not been respected. This had made them feel uncomfortable, so they had moved on at the earliest opportunity.

Our example person found it helpful to examine their values. They realised that now they had to keep being aware of the values they identified and, through the next few weeks, check the validity of their decisions. (Interestingly, this linked with their 'robust intelligent analysis' value!)

The Law of Mirroring

This exercise on identifying values in others is based on the Law of Mirroring. There have been many psychological studies that affirm that the world around you acts as a mirror for your mind. Freud, for example, talks of projection in which you see different qualities, characteristics and personal aspects of your own self reflected in others.

In your everyday life, when you see something that you do or do not like in others, you tend to accept or reject them. The Law of Mirroring claims that, in some way, an aspect that you see in another also exists within you.

Obviously, with many of the people in this example, they have never actually met, so cannot say they really know them; in reality, what you're likely doing in this exercise is projecting your own values onto others. When this situation occurs, you're superimposing your projected vision of yourself on the physical image of that person captured by your own senses.

Using this law of mirroring is often a quick way to understand ourselves. Here we were trying to understand if we were projecting our values.

The Johari Window

Here, a concept known as the Johari Window, developed by Joseph Luft and Harrington Ingham in 1955, is useful. It was designed to help people understand the relationships between themselves and others. When looking at the window, we realise that when we look at ourselves there is an important area to discover – what others see in us – our 'blind spot' and, with any of the exercises, good practice is to check what you have learned with others who may have a different view from yours.

	What I know	What I don't know
What others know	Public self	Blind spot
What they don't know	Private self	Subconscious

The Johari Window

Source: Luft, J. and Ingham, H. (1955) 'The Johari Window, a Graphic Model of Interpersonal Awareness', Proceedings of the Western Training Laboratory in Group Development, Los Angeles.

It is a very good idea to identify a group of up to six people you respect who you are going to ask to help you on this journey. Share the results of your exercises with them or aspects of them where you feel they can help most.

Most people we speak to on this subject feel embarrassed to ask for help – but we can assure you that, in virtually every case, those you ask will be extremely happy to help.

Exercise 11
Checking your values

- -

We have identified our values and, through that process, have an understanding of what values we project. Now we need to make sure others can see those values by checking with them.

We are using the Johari Window to check what others see in us that we do too.

Often, this exercise also uncovers values others see but we don't, as well as what we see and they don't.

For this exercise, ask your group of people to identify three to five values they believe you have. Normally, they will tell you stories about events they remember where your values were evident.

It is important to jot these down and also to incorporate them into other exercises like your lifeline, if you think them important to remember.

Then look at the results from your group.

- Are there similarities in the values they see in you?
- How do the values they expressed fit with what you have identified?
- Do their identification of values expand or focus in on particular values you believe are important to you?

- -

The importance of context

Think about organisations where you have worked and your colleagues at that time. Can you see now why they were right or wrong for you? Think about the work you are doing now. You may feel really satisfied that you 'fit' the role you are doing or know that there is a mismatch between your work and your values.

Maybe the *work* is right for you but the *situation/context* is wrong?

Some people do well for years in a particular role. Then there is a takeover and the culture changes in the wrong way for them. Is it them or is it the situation they find themselves in?

In many cases, people make the mistake of thinking they are no longer any good at a role when actually the context has changed, and they have not realised that that change of context has created a problem for them. You hear of people saying, 'I'm a has-been', 'I realise I'm out of date or too old', when, in fact, they are perfectly good at *what* they do, the problem is that the context has changed and made them feel inadequate.

It frequently turns out that the work is aligned with their talents, just as before.

The problem is there is a clash between their values and the values of the new organisation that has taken over.

This is why so many organisations spend a lot of time on understanding the culture they want to create to attract those that hold similar values.

You have to consider yourself in terms of whether the environment you are working in supports you enough or is too toxic to tolerate. Some people can tolerate a culture that attacks their values but draw the line when they realise what they are doing goes against them.

If you discover that your values clash with the work itself, it is worth considering any changes you could make.

Remember, the strongest personal brands are developed by people doing what they love, in a situation/context that nurtures and is compatible with their values.

If you want to look more deeply into your values, you can also consider doing the same exercise but rather than *people*, think about the *things* you admire. Write down all the things in your life that have had some meaning for you. They can range from your favourite teddy bear to an interest in architecture to the latest camera or an amazing sunset. The qualities you admire in these things will add another dimension to your values.

Fulfilling your potential

In many cases, the positive qualities we admire in others are those we have yet to acknowledge in ourselves. We may even have suppressed them for some reason. As we have already said, we can 'project' these qualities onto other people without realising they are our own values. Doing these exercises is not about simply uncovering our values and acknowledging them, it is also about standing back and thinking how this knowledge can help us to fulfil our potential.

Once you acknowledge this, you can reclaim each quality and make it your own. If you admire people who are highly creative, it may be time for you to be more creative. If you admire people who are influential, it may be time for you to exert more influence. You do not have to give up your current job or business. You can start right now, exactly where you are.

The following exercise will help you examine this more closely.

Exercise 12
What holds me back from being the best version of myself?

- -

Look back at what you wrote for the previous exercises. Look at the values you have uncovered both by yourself and those for which you have asked for help.

In most cases, it is our limiting beliefs that hold us back from being the best version of ourselves, so make some time to sit back and think about what your support group has said to you in terms of the values they see in you.

It might be time to ask them the two very important questions that we use to give really useful 360° feedback to people.

These questions need to be asked in a conversation so the recipient does not have time to think – but comes out with their immediate thoughts.

The first question you ask them is:

- What makes me stand out from the crowd – what do you see in me that draws you to me?

The second question is:

- What holds me back from being the best version of myself – both personally and the context I am in?

This second question incorporates both your limiting beliefs as well as the context within which you are working, e.g. an unsupportive boss or a team who does not see your value to the organisation . . . a culture that does not allow you to shine.

This exercise links with both the lifeline exercise as well as those that follow next when looking at your talents.

Key takeaways

- Your values are what you believe you stand for.
- The Johari Window helps us to understand what others see in us that we do not and also what we see in us that they do not.
- You can now see how the context you find yourself in is either positive or negative as it either reflects positive or negative values that you hold.
- To realise our potential, we need to be clear about our values because, by knowing them clearly, you will be able to identify with the right people and organisations.

chapter 8

Your talents

The dictionary provides two definitions of the word *talent*. The first is a natural ability to do something well. The second is a person of exceptional ability. However, the word talent is sometimes used to describe 'anyone we employ and therefore have to manage'. And some organisations even have 'talent pools'. We prefer to stick to the dictionary. Your brand should be based on your talents – the things you naturally do well, that stand out about you.

What are your talents?

If your brand is a building, your talents are how the building is used effectively. It is about how it stands out from others. It is about its usefulness.

Talents emerge at any time from early childhood onwards. Education can help you discover them. The words *educate* and *education* are derived from a Latin verb meaning *to draw out*. The educator draws out something that is already within you. With training and experience, a talent can be developed into one or more *skills*.

Ironically, since our talents come naturally to us, it is easy to neglect them. There is something in our education system that ignores natural talents and concentrates on developing skills that we do not have. This can lead to an emphasis on focusing on weaknesses instead of strengths.

We are conditioned to value what we have to work hard at achieving.

Because our innate talents are often unseen, we want to spend time considering these. Exercise 12 at the end of the previous chapter might have already made you think about what others see as your talents that you did not notice yourself.

Your talents manifest themselves in what you enjoy most and do best. If you think back to when you really enjoyed your work – and did a great job – you will probably find you were using your talents effectively. You were able to do what was needed and everything fell into place. It may have seemed effortless. People often become immersed in their talents and lose track of time.

As we have already said, psychologist Mihaly Csikszentmihalyi describes these optimal experiences as *flow*. You are likely to experience *flow* when you combine your talents in ways you find meaningful and stretch them to the limits of your ability. *Flow experiences* help you identify your talents. They also show you the ways of using your talents that you find most fulfilling.

Identifying your talents

The best way to identify your talents is to examine what you have done well in the past. Ask people who know you well to help you. They will remember you in different situations.

Please note that talents are not the same as skills. Talents are innate. You are born with them and cannot change them. For this reason, they are sometimes described as *gifts*. Over time, you can develop skills that are based on your talents. Examples of talents include:

- Using humour to lighten the mood of a group.
- Easily spotting a mistake in a page of words or numbers.
- Capturing the essence of an argument in a few simple words.
- Capturing the hearts and minds of a group of people engaged in a task.

This brings us to the next exercise.

Exercise 13
Uncovering your talents

- -

(a) Reflect on your life story (Exercise 1) and identify at least five occasions that you recall as *high points* or *peak experiences*. (It doesn't matter how old you were when these high points occurred.) These are memories of times that gave you a great sense of pleasure or achievement. They are highly *meaningful* for you. List them in the spaces below. Take them from different areas of your life, including your childhood, education, work and leisure pursuits.

1 . . . .

2 . . . .

3 . . . .

4 . . . .

5 . . . .

6 . . . .

7 . . . .

If you recall more than seven high points, write the extra ones down, too. The more high points you have on the sheet of paper in front of you, the easier it will be to identify themes emerging from them. Be careful not to select events just because you consider them socially acceptable or likely to impress others. Choose those that are meaningful for *you*.

(b) For each high point, ask yourself:

- Which talents did I use and enjoy using the most?
- With what kind of people?
- In what type of situation?

(c) Now list your talents, starting with those that give you the most energy when you use them.

1 . . . .

2 . . . .

3 . . . .

4 . . . .

5 . . . .

6 . . . .

7 . . . . etc.

Are there any common themes connecting your high points? If so, write them down.

- -

Now, also look back on the low points in your life.

These are just as important as you recognise how you used talents you have to overcome obstacles or support yourself in difficult situations.

Go through the same process above with your 'high' points with these 'low' points.

This is an open-ended exercise. As you continue through the exercises in this book, further high and low points will emerge. Sometimes, those you had forgotten turn out to be particularly significant. It is important to ask people who have known you at different stages of your life for their views. The support group who has already helped you will be useful to engage with on this exercise too. They may remember experiences that you had forgotten.

When looking at your high and low points, where are you now in terms of feeling good or bad about where you are?

If you are feeling either flat or negative about your chosen profession or business, it is worth asking yourself whether you are working in the right area. High and low points can provide clues about other ways of applying your talents more enjoyably and profitably. Equally, if all your high points are in the distant past, it is worth asking yourself whether the path you have taken recently is right for you. Maybe there is another that would suit you better.

Once you've completed the exercise, take a moment to reflect. How do you feel about where you have come from and where you are going? What are the underlying themes? We will discuss these in later chapters.

We strongly encourage you to complete this exercise, as your reflections help you to clarify how your talents support your brand.

An example

This is what our example person discovered:

(a) Reflect on your life and identify seven occasions that you recall as *high points* or *peak experiences*.

   1 Working on a local farm from the age of seven. This was where I discovered my love of horse riding.

➤

2 Playing football and becoming captain of the school team, while doing fairly badly in my studies.

3 Having scraped into university to study history, suddenly beginning to enjoy my work and graduating in the top quartile.

4 Taking a year off to work as a volunteer on a project in East Africa.

5 Getting my first job in banking.

6 The successful project that put me on the fast track for promotion.

7 Developing a computer program that transformed how people worked.

Based on these seven high points, this person identified some key themes running through the talents that they both enjoyed and used the most. They are shown below. They realised that they naturally used their talents in situations where they felt they could make a difference. They particularly enjoyed working with intellectual people, in situations where their understanding of people and their talent for persuasion were valued.

Here are their talents ranked in descending order of importance to them:

1 Examining a complex situation and identifying the simplest solution

2 Listening carefully and persuading people to take the appropriate action

3 Identifying people's strengths and weaknesses

4 Building confidence within teams

5 Identifying patterns of behaviour that cause problems

6 Taking measured risks that raise his level of confidence.

These six talents are based on our example's peak experiences from the age of seven. Like many of us, they have certain talents that they *cannot stop* using. They have a deeply ingrained habit of solving other people's problems. When they looked back over the high points in their life, the theme of solving problems was always there. They love analysing complex situations and then devising practical solutions.

We encourage you to do this exercise thoroughly.

It will show you 'what you do' and 'how you do it'. One of the many benefits is that you will have a collection of stories you can tell other people to explain how you use your talents (even if you do not use the word *talents* when talking to them). Stories are particularly useful in an interview. As the saying goes: 'Facts tell. Stories sell.'

Most of the time, you may illustrate your talents by talking about high points that have occurred during your work. It is interesting to note fewer people are prepared to talk honestly about low points that have also made them the person they are today. By being this transparent with people, it engenders trust and will certainly make you stand out against other people who hold back from being honest.

In interviews, there is often a question about your weaknesses. Many people 'make up' a weakness that also shows a strength but is not really true. Any experienced interviewer will be able to see there is a problem, or at least sense something they do not trust.

Working on your lifeline to identify both your talents and what we call 'understrengths' is important to your understanding of *Brand You*.

The worry you might have about your understrengths being used as a reason not to hire you actually is false. Anyone interviewing you and only looking at what they consider weaknesses rather than what you can contribute probably shows the organisation you are applying to join may be the wrong one for you.

Another way people stand out in the interview process is they tell stories about talents from their childhood so that the interviewer can see how that talent has been developed over time – something few candidates think of doing. For example, an entrepreneur might talk about a business they set up at school. A musician might describe their first performance at the age of five.

Some people have one talent that makes them stand out. However, for most of us, it is a *combination* of talents that makes us unique. It is how we use them together that allows others to notice our brand.

Exercise 14
Your combination of talents

- -

Look again at the first exercise and pick again the seven occasions of high and low points in your life and at the list of talents you wrote down in the last exercise.

Look at each occasion and ask yourself:

- How did I combine my talents on those occasions?
- What were the specific talents I was using at the time of those events?
- Are there underlying talents that are emerging as I look at the seven occasions I have picked out?
- If I go back to the lifeline and pick out another, do the same talents also appear there?
- Looking back on my life, which two or three times have I felt myself the most powerful in terms of using all my talents to their optimum?
- Are there talents I realise I should be using more?
- Does my situation allow me to utilise all my talents or use only some?
- Overall, what percentage of my talents am I using?

- Is this enough for me?
- How far have you combined your talents in ways that you really enjoyed?
- Looking at the future, what talents do you want to develop even more?

- -

Our example often combined their talent for identifying people's strengths and weaknesses with their talent for building confidence within teams.

Exercise 15
Integration of purpose, values and talents
- -

Once you have completed the talents exercises, it is time to reflect over the 11 exercises you have worked on in this first part of the book. If you can, bring your answers together in one place.

Then give yourself some time to see the links between them and work on exercises that feel weak or uncomfortable. The key is to be able to look at all the exercises so far and be able to say, 'This is good enough for the moment,' recognising that things will change in the future.

You should be satisfied that you have much more clarity on your personal unique and authentic brand.

- -

Key takeaways
- -

- Understanding your talents is important so that you can see potential ways in which you can differentiate yourself from others and uncover your unique and authentic brand.

- You uncover your talents by looking back on your life and interrogating both the high and low points in your life story.

- Examine how you combine your talents to stand out.

- At this point, you can integrate all the exercises you have worked on so far to create a clear picture of who you are, how you operate and what you do well – your authentic brand should be emerging.

chapter 9

Using archetypes to develop your brand

By now, you will have spent some time thinking about your purpose, values and talents. Our next task is to enhance your *brand identity*, which brings them all together. It consists of the symbols, signs, language, images and colours that distinguish you from other people in your line of work.

In Chapter 2, we discussed using the concept of archetypes, extensively used in product marketing, where it is used to create an immediate sense of familiarity with customers.

Archetypes are used to connect with people on a deeper level, tapping into their emotions and getting them excited about you.

Customers rarely make rational decisions alone – they are always guided by their emotions and that is why just presenting the facts of who you are and what you do is often not enough. Archetypes help customers instinctively understand certain things about you.

Psychoanalyst Carl Jung developed archetypes after noticing certain personality traits repeated in various stories throughout history. He theorised that humans use symbolism to understand the world, and that recognition of the qualities of the different archetypes was rooted in our collective unconscious.

David Ogilvy, often referred to as the 'father of advertising', said we must build:

'Sharply defined personalities for their brands and stick to those personalities year after year. It is the total personality of the brand rather than any trivial product difference that decides its position in the market place.'

A distinct, authentic brand identity will help you attract the right employers, clients and colleagues. It will also help them recommend you to others.

The power of archetypes

Archetypes can give your brand a clear meaning, by communicating *how* you do things. The Greek root of the word *archetype* means *first-moulded*. Carl Jung believed that we have a universal shared unconscious out of which archetypes emerge as forms or images that everyone recognises. These forms or images have the same meaning for people wherever they are in the world. We instinctively recognise archetypes in ourselves, other people, objects, situations and organisations, whether or not we are aware that we are doing so.

In 2001, Margaret Mark and Carol S. Pearson published *The Hero and the Outlaw – Building Extraordinary Brands Through the Power of Archetypes*. They showed how Jungian archetypes enabled companies to manage the *meaning* of branded products and services. They also suggested that archetypes could be applied to *personal* brands, which is what we will do in this book.

Archetypes can be extremely powerful. We have presented this material to audiences of many nationalities. They all recognise the same archetypes.

We can learn a lot from leading actors and musicians. As Mark and Pearson point out:[1]

'**Superstars in the film and entertainment industry, and the agents who manage them, understand that their continued popularity does not hinge simply on the quality or success of the films they make or the visibility they attain. Rather, it depends on creating, nourishing and continuously reinterpreting a unique and compelling identity or "meaning".**'

Whatever your line of work, you can use a similar approach, in line with your unique purpose, values and talents.

How archetypes work

Our starting point is that you have a purpose. Developing a powerful brand involves *projecting* your purpose to the outside world. Archetypes can help you do this by representing your purpose in a form that everyone recognises. If your behaviour is consistent with your natural archetype(s), your brand will take on a meaning that increases your appeal to people who want what you have to offer.

Below is a description of the archetypes in Mark and Pearson's model. We have modified the titles and used international examples where possible. As you read the paragraphs below, one may stand out as *your* archetype. Others may fit someone you know.

Please note that we do not expect you to fit into a box or *become* any of the archetypes below. Instead, you *evoke* the archetype in your work. The verb *to evoke* is derived from the Latin verb *evocare*, meaning *to call forth*. When you evoke an archetype, your behaviour and the way you present yourself call it forth in the minds of other people and yourself. We will come back to the question of *how* you do this. In the meantime, here are the archetypes. You may notice that some seem more prevalent in certain occupations but not others.

The Caregiver

The Caregiver archetype is altruistic, compassionate and nurturing – motivated by a desire to help others and protect them from harm. They provide reassurance, advice and support to ensure the wellbeing of others. Examples include Mother Teresa, Florence Nightingale and Desmond Tutu. Similarly, celebrities can represent the Caregiver archetype by using their platform to shine a light on issues like poverty, illnesses such as AIDS and education. For instance, Bono from the band U2, Elton John and Dolly Parton.

The World Wildlife Fund (WWF) is an example of this archetype, working to help people and nature thrive, and communities across the globe conserve their natural resources. Charitable organisations such as The Salvation Army and the Samaritans also evoke this archetype by listening to and helping vulnerable adults. Likewise, doctors, nurses and social workers as well as human resource personnel can often evoke the caregiver.

These are obvious places where caregiving is understood but, in any role, particularly when you are looking after other people in a management role, this archetype might help you to make your brand visible to others. In leadership roles, 'trust' is important, and there should be some aspect of caregiving present.

The Creator

The Creator archetype is about innovation and creativity. It's often seen in writers, artists, composers, inventors and entrepreneurs. They have daydreams and flashes of inspiration that they translate into reality. The Creator is about self-expression, rather than fitting in. When the Creator archetype is active in people, they often feel *compelled* to create or innovate – they look for alternative ways of solving problems. They have a vision that must take physical form, and they want to create something of lasting value. Examples include Leonardo da Vinci, Wolfgang Amadeus Mozart and Thomas Edison, who invented the first long-lasting light bulb. Marie Curie, the first female winner of the Nobel Prize for her work in radioactivity, discovering polonium and radium is another example. Less well-known but equally important are people like Dr Shirley Jackson, the first Black woman to graduate with a PHD whose research in telecommunications led to the invention of fibre-optic cables, and Grace Hopper, who co-invented COBOL – the first universal programming language. More recent Creators will include Mark Zuckerberg, the founder of Facebook; Elon Musk, the serial technology entrepreneur; Grayson Perry, the artist; Edward Enninful, editor of Vogue magazine; and Zaha Hadid, the architect.

Companies who evoke this archetype include the Chinese conglomerate Haier and the Indian conglomerate Mahindra Group who have created and diversified different services as their companies grew.

The Explorer

The Explorer – unsurprisingly – wants to explore. Explorers want to maintain freedom and independence. They are naturally curious about everything. There is an underlying feeling of dissatisfaction and restlessness. The exploration can be geographical, as it was for Christopher Columbus, Marco Polo and *Star Trek*. However, the joy of discovery can also extend to new products and services. Explorers have an underlying desire to find out what fits with their inner needs and preferences. They are always searching for 'something more' but are never satisfied with the outcome. Jeanne Baret, the first woman to circumnavigate the world, and Annie Smith Peck, one of the greatest mountaineers of the nineteenth century, are examples of the Explorer. The actor Ewan McGregor evokes the Explorer in his motorcycle journeys. Richard Branson evokes the Explorer when he travels thousands of miles in a hot-air balloon or invests millions in space technology. Francis Crick and James Watson, the molecular biologists, evoked the Explorer when they discovered the structure of DNA. David Attenborough, often described as a British 'national treasure', known for his world travels exploring the natural environment, evokes the Explorer archetype.

Organisations such as Red Bull, 'giving you wings', evoking thrilling new experiences through their advertising and NASA, who conducts space exploration, are examples of this archetype.

In business, those who 'look outside the box' or have alternative points of view based on their curiosity to find new ways to deal with old problems are highly valued.

The Hero

The Hero acts courageously to improve a situation. They are attracted to chaos because it provides an opportunity for heroism. Heroes stand up for what they believe in. There are fictional heroes such as Superman, Wonder Woman and James Bond. Real-life examples include Nelson Mandela and Aung San Suu Kyi, the dissident who has spent much of her life under house arrest. Amelia Earhart evoked the Hero when she became the first woman to fly solo across the Atlantic. Police, ambulance drivers and firefighters can also evoke the Hero. A hero could also be KSI – whose videos on YouTube have surpassed 4 billion views and who has more than 19 million subscribers – who rose to fame after publishing videos of himself and gaining attention as a gamer musician and boxer. He continues to inspire young people to follow their dreams by showing that, by building on your various talents, multiple careers are possible. Lesser-known heroes are people like Basira Popul, a dedicated polio worker in Afghanistan helping to vaccinate children and bring an end to this crippling disease. There are many unsung heroes who have supported people all around the world during the COVID-19 pandemic.

Some executives evoke the hero when they turn a company around and prevent it from going into liquidation. They may even describe potential disasters in detail to those around them; it adds to the thrill of pulling through and making everything right.

Other business executives like Mohamed Yunus, founder of the Grameen Bank, developed pioneering concepts of microcredit and microfinance to help provide access to finance for small businesses in India. A hero for the worker was Dan Price, CEO of Gravity Payments. He cut his salary so that he could pay all his staff a minimum wage of $70,000 (the average salary had been $48,000).

Whistleblowing is in the news around the world where individuals have taken a stand while potentially causing themselves great harm. They have taken their stand not for themselves but because they believe wrongdoing needs to be exposed; they also evoke this archetype. Individuals who come to mind are Julian Assange of Wikileaks, who published leaked documents that had an impact on political news. As well as a hero, some people may also regard him as an outlaw. Cynthia Cooper, who, as vice-president of internal audit at telecom giant WorldCom, investigated and alerted the board to accounting irregularities that had resulted in $3.8 billion in overstated revenue. In Florida, COVID data tracker Rebekah Jones is another example, who says she was terminated from her government position for refusing to manipulate the data to paint a rosier picture of Florida's COVID crisis.[2]

The Innocent

The Innocent is about fostering purity, goodness and simplicity. They have strong moral values and strive for authenticity. The Latin and Old French root of the word *innocent* means 'no harm'. Their primary aim is to create happiness, perhaps even the experience of paradise. For example, the Dove Brand has stated that it cares about how their products are manufactured and the ingredients that go into them, as well as their carbon footprint and sustainability of their products.

Innocent Drinks, founded in 1999, now sells more than 2 million smoothies each week. The ingredients are fruit and fruit juice, with no 'weird stuff' – in other words, no artificial ingredients. Examples of the Innocent archetype from Hollywood include Tom Hanks in the role of Forrest Gump. Disney evokes the innocent in films such as *Bambi* and *Snow White*. Books such as *The Little Prince* by Antoine de Saint-Exupéry and Charlie Mackesy's *The Boy, the Mole, the Fox and the Horse* are good examples of this. A dietician or someone who helps you stop smoking could also evoke this archetype. Monks, nuns and holy people in many cultures evoke the Innocent. This archetype is also known as the Child.

Some business people evoke the Innocent, at least for a while. The innocent is that person in a meeting who asks simple questions that make a big impact; they may be unassuming but their ability to see a simple clear solution in complex situations makes them stand out. An example is Rosa Parks. She refused to give up her seat to a white person on a bus, but didn't intend to make an impactful difference, all she wanted was to go home in peace. It was a simple act, but led to her being regarded as the first lady of the African American civil rights movement.

The Jester

On the surface, the Jester usually has a good time, enjoying the moment. However, they often have something important to say and are surprisingly versatile and complex. They are not simply the fool – there is a lot going on in the background. The Jester always knows the truth and know who the people are who have ulterior motives. They are often at the centre of things, using their charisma to ask searching questions that challenge and provoke, and they often play the role of devil's advocate. This archetype suited consumer brand Ben & Jerry's ice-cream company. Fun and humour pervade the brand's activities, including its campaign to help combat global warming:

> **'Ben & Jerry's Climate Change College is a launch pad for 18–30 year olds who agree with us that ice caps, just like ice cream, are best kept frozen.'**

Jesters say things that others dare not and can be highly influential. Executive assistants or chiefs of staff often play this role, where an important figure has surrounded themselves with those who are not prepared to challenge their decisions; the Jester will do so in a way that dares to tell the truth. Jesters are risk takers and do not always use humour to make their case, as in the case of many activists. An example is Jo Brand, the English comedian, who was censored by the BBC for comments made during the Radio 4 programme *Heresy* designed to push boundaries. In Hollywood, examples of jesters include Melissa McCarthy as Megan in *Bridesmaids*, Jim Carey in *The Mask* and Rebel Wilson, the Australian actress, comedian, writer, singer and producer.

Jesters also provoke other people, exposing their prejudices. Sacha Baron Cohen did this as Borat in the film *Cultural Learnings of America for Make Benefit Glorious Nation of Kazakhstan*.

One of our former colleagues attributes his success to playing the role of the Jester: he says that, 'Clients like being challenged. They also want to compare themselves. However, I have to be discreet. Much of what I do goes on behind the curtain. If I find out they are doing something new in the US, I send them a message right away, to suggest I help them do the same thing in Europe. I win lots of business by crossing the bridge to their castle and gently provoking them.'

The Lover

The Lover wants to find and give love, and experience pleasure. This archetype is concerned with staying close to the people, surroundings and activities they love. There is an archetypal yearning for true love in many Hollywood stars. For instance, many see the fictional character James Bond, also known as 007, as appealing in terms of his manner and attitude, as much as his physicality.

It is also seen in products such as perfume, chocolate and ice cream. Fashion models, pop stars and writers of popular fiction often evoke the Lover.

These people remind us that love is one of the most important attributes to bring to decision making, ensuring people realise that the basic need to love and be loved needs to be considered in all decisions. They value togetherness, connection and collaboration.

One of the most famous business people to evoke the Lover is Coco Chanel, who was known both as a dress designer and as the mistress of famous and wealthy men. Sales of her perfume, Chanel No. 5, rocketed once it received the free endorsement of Marilyn Monroe. Chanel had a keen sense of her personal brand. When asked why she did not marry the Duke of Westminster, she replied: 'There have been several Duchesses of Westminster. There is only one Chanel.'

An example of an organisation that evokes the Lover archetype is The Elders, a group of independent global leaders working together for peace, justice, human rights and a sustainable planet. Even some terms such as 'Ubuntu', a Zulu philosophy meaning 'humanity' that is sometimes translated as 'I am because we are', can evoke the lover.

The Magician

The role of the Magician is fundamentally to *transform*. One of the underlying themes is discovering the laws of the universe in order to make things happen. The Magician pays attention to hunches and meaningful coincidences. Harry Potter, the star of the eponymous novels, is an obvious example. They are normally a bearer of knowledge that helps others transform, and they are the ones that turn ideas into reality. Google can be seen evoking this archetype, offering a route to any answer you need. Their stated mission is organise all of the information in our world and make it accessible to all.

The Magician often appears in advertisements for cleaning products, with taglines such as 'Bang! And the dirt is gone!'

For many people, Steve Jobs evokes the Magician. At Apple, he constantly had ideas that transformed people's lives. He was sometimes described as 'The Wizard of Cupertino'. In the 1800s, Ada Lovelace is another example. She was barely known in history, yet she was considered the first ever computer programmer. She was strongly interested in scientific developments and had a desire to create a mathematical model for how the brain gives rise to thoughts and nerves to feelings.

Beulah Loise Henry, the prolific inventor of ice-cream freezing, can openers, etc., is another. She said, 'I invent because I can't help it, new things just thrust themselves on me.' Hermione Granger (from *Harry Potter*) is a great example of a Magician, and not just because she can do magic. Right from her introduction, her power is magnified through her dedication to her studies.

Many leaders evoke the Magician when they create a vision that links individuals' personal dreams to the corporate purpose, making everyone involved believe that they can do better and achieve superior performance.

For most people, the magician archetype is that person you go to when you want dramatic change.

The Ordinary Person

Ordinary People simply want to belong and ensure people work together and are OK as they are. They want to fit in and connect with others. Entertainers such as Pink in the USA and Ed Sheeran and Adele in the UK evoke this archetype. In the corporate world it is seen in executives who have *the common touch*. Ordinary People enjoy self-deprecating humour, demonstrating that they do not take themselves too seriously. They often watch popular sports and have a connection with people that cross social boundaries. Successful sales people frequently evoke the Ordinary Person. When they first contact an organisation that could buy their product or service, they chat and build rapport with people at all levels, from the receptionist to the office manager and the boss's personal assistant. This helps every stage of the sales process to go smoothly.

Stelios Haji-Ioannou, the founder of easyJet and many other businesses, demonstrated the fact that you *evoke* an archetype rather than *become* it. Despite his wealthy upbringing, he is known for giving the man and woman in the street what they want at an affordable price. Having made his name with his low-cost airline, his subsequent ventures include easyCruise, easyCar, easyHotel and easyOffice.

The IKEA brand is a classic case of this archetype in practice, offering everyday home products for the average person.

The Outlaw

The Outlaw or Rebel is a maverick who rebels and breaks the rules. Similar in some ways to the Creator, they are differentiated by their aggressiveness and preparedness to break any rule that gets in their way. They disrupt the status quo. Outlaw brands in music include the Rolling Stones, Madonna and the Sex Pistols.

For many years, technology company Apple evoked the Outlaw. Its logo of an apple with a bite taken out of it recalls Adam and Eve, who ate the forbidden fruit and were cast out of the Garden of Eden. In the early days, this was aligned with Apple's role as the computer manufacturer that challenged the Ruler, namely IBM. It initially made the distinction between itself and the 'suits' who rule the companies where they work. Interestingly, this seems to be changing as Apple becomes a more 'Ruler' brand.

Harley-Davidson is about challenging the status quo and breaking out of routine, taking to the road.

Greta Thunberg, the Swedish environmental activist, is known for challenging world leaders to take immediate action on climate change.

Entrepreneurs often evoke the Outlaw. They break with convention in order to start something new. For example, think of Uber and Airbnb.

The Ruler

The Ruler takes control, creating order out of chaos. Rulers *have* to organise things. They are both powerful and dominating. Alexander the Great evoked this archetype, as did Margaret Thatcher when she was Britain's prime minister. The Ruler wants to be the best, create a successful and prosperous family or company, but fears being overthrown. They can also be working quietly in the background, known for their attention to detail and perfectionist personality.

They want wealth and success in everything they do. SAP, the German software company, evokes the Ruler by helping people who run large organisations to keep things under control.

Rolex is a leading watch brand and has always portrayed itself as 'the best'. It knows that people wear its brand to prove they are the elite, the leaders in what they do.

The Sage

The Sage helps people to understand their world. They are wise, reflective, thoughtful and healing. They are the person in an organisation that knows it fully, either by being there for a long time, or because they have the big picture of the organisation's journey and what decisions went well or badly. They are used as trusted advisors, guides whose purpose is 'seeking out and sharing the truth'.

If you feel you are all about putting knowledge, truth and research above all else, then the following brand will resonate with you.

Plato and Confucius both evoked the Sage. They project the message that by studying you will gain a deeper understanding. Some companies, such as McKinsey, also embody this archetype by hiring highly educated people and training them in a particular way. McKinsey also publishes a journal, *The McKinsey Quarterly*.

In software technology companies, the head of software development sometimes evokes the Sage – they are the Expert. If they are highly knowledgeable rather than sales-oriented, it is reassuring for both customers and shareholders.

Both Oxford and Harvard Universities evoke this brand.

Identifying your archetypes

As we said earlier, none of us fits neatly into a box. You can see that there are overlaps between archetypes, such as the Magician and Sage, but you will probably either be more about transformation in your need for change, or wanting to develop change from a healing point of view. During the course of a day, you might evoke the Caregiver, the Hero, the Ruler, the Jester, the Creator and the Lover. However, you will notice you are naturally inclined towards one archetype in your life. You will feel attracted to it. People who know you well will recognise it in you.

Here, it will be useful to use that group of people who helped you uncover your 'blind spot'. It will be interesting to see if your archetype is well defined in their eyes or they see different archetypes in you. If the latter is the case, there is a need to identify which archetype you favour most.

You will build a much stronger brand if you evoke one archetype – or possibly two – consistently. Consciously or unconsciously, people want to know what you stand for. They also value consistency. If you consistently evoke a particular archetype, they will feel they know who you are and can trust you to behave in a certain way. They will feel safe around you. They will know what they can ask you to do, if the need arises. All of this makes it easier for them to choose you or recommend you to others.

As we mentioned earlier, you *evoke* an archetype rather than become it. For example, a care worker may naturally have some traits of the 'Caregiver' archetype. However, one we know is seen much more as a Magician – it is amazing how they can help depressed elderly people to enjoy life again.

At the other end of the spectrum, a CEO we know has moved countries and is leading a new top team in a different culture with different issues to face. He and those who know him see the combination of 'ruler' and 'explorer' archetypes are what set him apart from other CEOs.

One might assume the Ruler is naturally the archetype for CEOs and those who run teams of people, just as the care worker we mentioned naturally evokes the 'Caregiver'.

Actually, this is not always true and to develop a strong brand, having a strong archetype that is not obvious for the role you are taking helps you stand out from the crowd. If you were recruiting for a CEO or care worker and they all exhibited the expected archetype, it would be difficult to differentiate them. When asking your group for their view on you, they may notice many more archetypes that you evoke that are *unusual*.

Life might be simpler if each of us needed to evoke only one archetype consistently at work. However, many people naturally evoke two of them. You may need at least two – one that allows others to *trust* you in your role, and another that helps to *set you apart* from others that do similar jobs.

Here are some examples:

- The product engineer of a large manufacturing company evokes the Ordinary Person when they build relationships with their staff, including journalists, sales people, creatives and others from a wide range of backgrounds. They evoke the Magician while they are transforming the company, helping it to succeed in a new environment.

- A business development director employed by another large company evokes the Explorer while they search for suitable businesses to acquire. They also evoke the Creator when they draw up plans to launch new ventures inhouse.

- A doctor evokes the Magician when they prescribe medicine that helps people recover from sudden illnesses. They evoke the Caregiver when recommending changes in their patient's diet and lifestyle that will protect them from relapses.

- A comedian evokes the Jester and the Ordinary Person when they make jokes about themselves and their circumstances. People relate to them and what they are saying. People hear the funny comments on politicians, for example, but are also aware the humour is making light of serious issues.

- Barack Obama evoked the Ordinary Person and the Hero when he campaigned to become president of the United States in 2008 and 2012. His campaign successfully emphasised his upbringing in a broken home. The financial crisis helped him to evoke the Hero at a time when voters were already looking for someone who would save them from disaster.

Madonna: a case study in combining two archetypes

Madonna is recognised as the world's best-selling female recording singer of all time by the Guinness World Records, having sold over 300 million albums. She was the third of six children born to Italian–American parents. Madonna's father worked in the Chrysler car factory near Detroit. Her mother died when Madonna was six and she was brought up as a Roman Catholic, which has strongly influenced her music and her imagery. She has both acknowledged and rebelled against her religion throughout her career.

Madonna followed David Bowie's example by continuously changing her image, thus maintaining people's interest in her and her music. However, in terms of archetypes, she has consistently evoked both the Lover and the Outlaw. As she once said: 'When I was tiny my grandmother used to beg me not to go with boys, to love Jesus and be a good girl. I grew up with two images of women: the Virgin and the whore.'

In the 1980s, a generation of young women identified with her, as someone who fought her way to the top in a man's world while managing to remain rebellious and attractive. By marketing herself as a sex symbol, she attracted attention from a male audience at the same time. Some of the key events in her career show how she has built a powerful brand:

- Her strong style enabled her to cross boundaries between audiences. Her music is played in both gay and straight clubs in the United States and appeals to a variety of ethnic groups.

- The launch of MTV, the 24-hour music TV channel, and its imitators helped her to reach a much larger audience than would have been possible through touring alone. In early 1985, her second album and video *Like A Virgin* made her a fixture on MTV. Video enabled her to control her image carefully and occasionally borrow ideas from Hollywood films, inviting comparison with film stars of the past.
- She recorded other people's songs as well as her own, which helped her to produce high-quality work consistently.
- In 1990, sales of her compilation album *The Immaculate Collection* were boosted by the furore over the video of *Justify My Love,* which was banned by MTV and swiftly became a must-have item. By February 1991, it had become the first video short to sell more than 400,000 copies.
- Her popularity was enhanced by her film roles – winning a Golden Globe for Best Actress for her portrayal of Evita (1996).
- She also set up her company Maverick, with Maverick Records being one of the most successful artist-led labels in history.
- In the summer of 2006, she became the worldwide face of H&M, the clothing retailer, launching her own fashion line, *M by Madonna,* in March 2007.
- In 2008, *Billboard* magazine ranked Madonna at number two, behind *The Beatles,* on the *Billboard Hot 100 All-Time Top Artists,* making her the most successful solo artist in the history of the *Billboard* chart.
- Her philanthropy is well-known. By 2013, her 'Raising Malawi' charity had built 10 schools educating over 4,000 children and, by 2017, had also built a paediatric hospital there.
- Her 14th studio album, *Madame X* in 2019 (*NME* calling it 'bold and bizarre'), projects a rebellious and strong image.

Sources: Madonna – the Complete Guide to Her Music, by Rikky Rooksby (Omnibus Press)

As far as archetypes are concerned, the main thing is to identify one or two that suit you best – that attract you and make you feel most comfortable. Each of us draws upon other archetypes at various times. It does not matter, provided you are authentic. In other words, you consistently act in accordance with your values.

Distinguishing your archetypes

You do not have to evoke the same archetype(s) as the organisation where you work. For example, we know an all-day café that evokes the Innocent. The ingredients are pure and fresh. The Italian flat bread is baked on site. However, the founder embodies the Creator, as well as the Innocent. While they develop the recipes – and safeguard the purity of the brand – this is their third start-up. One day, they plan to spend more time on creative writing. It helps that their investors see both the Innocent and the Creator in them and value how the brand created has differentiated the café from others. They realise that the founder is intent on creating a profitable business as well as baking great bread.

Archetypes are not on a spectrum with two extremes, or a wheel consisting of opposites. Archetypes are simply different – and each of us evokes them all at some point. At the same time, we are attracted to certain archetypes that fit us best. It may, therefore, be useful to work for an organisation that evokes an archetype that is also prominent in you. For example, if your talents are in financial analysis and the Ruler archetype fits you well, you would probably find it satisfying to work for a Ruler-type organisation, such as a traditional bank. However, it is worth bearing in mind that different departments within the organisation will have a secondary archetype that relates to the work being done there. For example, the marketing department of a Caregiver insurance company might adopt a Jester approach to its advertising in a highly competitive market.

It is now time to identify *your* archetype(s). The following exercise will help you.

Exercise 16
Your archetypes

- -

Refer to the results of the exercises that you have recently completed in Chapters 5 and 6. Take another look at your top five values, your mission and your purpose. Do they suggest an archetype that you evoke naturally?

Show the description of the archetypes to your trusted colleagues and/or friends. Also include people you have known shorter term. Ask them which archetype(s) they identify in you. If you and they pick the same archetype(s), then you have a clear brand identity. If they pick a range of different archetypes, it means your brand is not yet clearly defined.

- -

An example

Our example was attracted to the Hero archetype above all others. They feel they work best that way and enjoy the challenge of doing things better than ever before. If a business is underperforming, they take great pleasure in making rapid improvements. They also evoke the Creator, with their emphasis on building lasting relationships and robust organisations.

You may be tempted to keep your options open by giving different messages to different people. However, by trying to appeal to every-one, you can fail to appeal strongly to *anyone*. Think of washing powder in your local supermarket. Some brands wash whiter than white; others keep your colours bright; some are designed to protect people with allergies. Each has a unique appeal. One will stand out as the best for the purpose you have in mind, while others blend into the background. No one wants a washing powder that may perhaps be quite good for something or other but doesn't solve your problem.

Nowadays, most of us face too many choices and have to process too much information, on a daily basis. Strong brands simplify our decisions and give us a feeling of certainty and reassurance.

In most product categories, the majority of people can remember only two or three leading brands. In cola beverages, it could be Coke or Pepsi. The same applies to people who are considering using your services. The clearer the image of what you do and what you stand for, the easier it will be for them to choose *you*. Once you have identified the archetype you evoke *naturally*, it is important to do so *consistently* in the eyes of your target market. You should be the first or second person they think of whenever they have a need. Many people want a choice of supplier, but they do not need more than two or three to choose from. Make sure you are one of them!

Your brand identity is like the exterior and interior of a building – they tell people what it is for and how things are done there. When you walk into a bank with Doric columns made of granite, you will probably have a feeling of solidity and security. The building evokes the Ruler, giving the impression that your savings are likely to be safe there. When someone walks into a health food store, they see the nuts, seeds and dried fruit in simple packaging. They notice the stripped pine shelving. The surroundings evoke the Innocent.

It is important for you to evoke your archetype consistently in everything you do and in all your presentation material. That way people will know what you stand for and will feel safe with you.

Key takeaways

- Archetypes can help you to develop a powerful brand by projecting your purpose to the outside world in a form that everyone recognises.

- If your behaviour is consistent with your natural archetype(s), your brand will be stronger and more appealing to people who want what you have to offer.

- People will know what you stand for if you consistently evoke a particular archetype.

Here is a summary of the archetypes we have discussed in this chapter:

The Caregiver	Helps and protects from harm – they are compassionate and nurturing
The Creator	Compelled to create and innovate – finding alternative ways to solve problems
The Explorer	Explores and discovers – they need freedom and independence to constantly search
The Hero	Acts courageously to put things right – they stand up for what they believe in
The Innocent	Seeks purity, goodness and happiness – they have strong moral values seeking simplicity and authenticity
The Jester	Has a good time but may convey a serious message – they know the truth and challenge and provoke
The Lover	Finds and gives love and sensual pleasure – they look for togetherness, connection and collaboration
The Magician	Transforms situations – through their knowledge they turn ideas into reality
The Ordinary Person	OK as they are; connects with others – working with them at the same level
The Outlaw	Rebels and breaks the rules – breaks conventions to get things done.
The Ruler	Takes control; creates order out of chaos – by being powerful and dominating
The Sage	Helps people to understand their world – looking to heal by seeking and sharing the truth

Notes

1 Mark, M. and Pearson, C. (2001) *The Hero and the Outlaw: Building Extraordinary Brands Through the Power of Archetypes* (Hardcover) McGraw Hill.

2 'Whistleblower of the Year Candidate – Rebekah Jones' (2020) available at: https://constantinecannon.com/whistleblower/ whistleblower-of-the-year-2020-rebekah-jones/.

part 3

Presenting your brand

Part 3 now moves from an internal focus, to link your unique and authentic brand to the external world of interest to you.

Moving from finding out who you are to presenting it to the world

So, we are now at the stage where we are moving from an inward focus on 'who I am' to an outward focus in terms of 'where am I going?'

We have looked at our purpose and identified our values and talents, and now we need to move to a point where we start to identify more clearly the strategy we want to adopt to ensure we are heading in the right direction in terms of the work we do.

In the past, you joined a company, worked for 30 years and retired with a gold watch, without even thinking about what you wanted to do. It was a job.

Today, we work in a completely different way, organisations are looking for talent, or potential talent, and individuals are prepared to move, on average, every three to four years to ensure they remain both marketable and energised by the work they undertake.

The process of clarifying the direction in which you want to go, however, is often done in a haphazard way. You may think 'I want a job called "x"', so, you look for job titles that 'fit' that without thinking of the wider context in which you might work.

At the same time, often you do not look for the right 'environment' . . . as long as the title is good, the benefits are OK, it is easy to travel to from home, and the pension and holidays are adequate, then that is good enough . . . Or is it?

We hope that, by going through the exercises to clarify, to some extent, 'who am I' in Part 1, you are in a much better position to see the opportunities available to you.

Now you understand your values, as an example, hopefully, you can see how important the environment around you is. You need it to be able to nurture you, to support you, to enable you to grow.

Yet, too many people accept what turns out to be a toxic environment, thinking that it is somehow a 'rite of passage' to suffer, to an extent, as part of the growing process.

While challenges are important to face, suffering, however, can simply hold you back from being the best you can be.

So, using what you have learned from the process so far in the creation of a robust strategy, going forward is a must.

This starts with the creation of documents both on and offline that shows to others your brand as clearly as possible.

However, in the first instance, we have to be clear about explaining what we do.

chapter 10

Explaining what you do

Now that you have completed the exercises in Part 2, you will be much clearer about your talents, your values, your purpose and your preferred archetype. The next question is, 'How will you use this knowledge to present yourself in your chosen field of work – where and what you do, knowing what you have uncovered about yourself in Part 2?'

In this chapter, we talk about creating a personal message, which has 'hooks' that encourage the listener to ask for more information from you by identifying your unique combination of talents, skills and experience.

We ask you to create a five-second statement of who you are and go on to use the GROW Model to clarify how you present yourself.

Your personal message

People often ask, 'What do you do?' One of the most typical responses is, 'How long have you got?' This is a typical response for those people who haven't reflected on who they are and therefore find it difficult to give a succinct answer.

Given that your listeners probably have limited time, it is essential to work out your personal message (an elevator pitch that will entice any hiring manager to want to know more about you) and put it across clearly and succinctly, just as you would if you were advertising a product or a business.

Your personal message can be described as the 'hook' that entices the listener to ask more about you. The hook allows you to explain aspects of your purpose, values, talents and experiences that you have identified. These elements help you to identify stories to explain the range of your capabilities and potentially resonate with the listener. They can be tailored depending on the context. Overall, the aim is to be authentic, concise and memorable – face to face, in print and online.

In conversation with the listener, you may identify how your archetype can be used to help you shape the language when inter-acting with them. You may need slightly different messages for dif-ferent situations.

You have many facets, just like a precious stone. Imagine you are in a dark room. Someone shines a spotlight on you from a particular direction, illuminating some of your facets but not others. Now they move the spotlight and shine it from another direction. Other facets stand out.

It is for you to decide which facets you are going to show to the outside world at any particular time. Doing the exercises in Part 2, it becomes easier for you to respond wherever the spotlight is shone, and helps to refine your brand that you will continue to develop in Part 3, where you are looking at how you can make the most impact with the outside world.

Your unique combination of talents, skills and experience

If asked to describe a friend or colleague, most people would say between two and four things about them – usually a mixture of their talents, skills and experience. It is often a rare combination. It may even be unique. If you can identify this combination about yourself and state it clearly, it will be easy for people to grasp what you have to offer and then share this with others. Many of the best opportunities come through word-of-mouth recommendation.

We discussed your talents in Chapter 8. Now it is time to talk about your skills and experience.

As you apply your talents to your career, you acquire experience and develop certain skills. A given talent could be developed into a variety of skills. For example, a talent for using words could be developed into the skills of a novelist, a translator, an editor, a screenplay writer, a journalist or a stockbroker, among many other occupations. A talent for spotting numerical patterns could be developed into the role of a statistician, a codebreaker, an actuary, an accountant or an investment analyst. You could apply a talent for organising people in the role of a chief executive, an army officer or a concert promoter. The more experience you gain of applying your talents in a particular way, the more valuable you become to employers and clients.

It is important that you recognise your skills and experience. The following exercise will help you.

Exercise 17
Your skills and experience
- -

Make a list of all the skills and types of experience you have acquired so far. They are likely to be rooted in your talents. The following questions will help you identify them:

- What have you studied?
- In which industries have you worked?

- Which languages do you speak?
- Have you ever spoken in public? To what kind of audience?
- At what stages in an organisation's life have you worked? Examples include start-up, rapid growth, consolidation, decline or liquidation.
- Which processes have you mastered? Examples include presenting in public, organising events, creating a strategy, launching a product, auditing a company, renovating a building, writing a book, running a change programme, running a manufacturing process, rewiring a house.
- What have you achieved that is measurable and could be relevant to a new employer or client?

- -

People who do this exercise often discover something they have overlooked. They also become much clearer about what they have to offer.

An example

Here are some of the skills and experiences of our example:

- Degree in business administration from the University of Hong Kong.
- Former president of the students' union.
- The youngest-ever brand manager at their previous employer, a major food company.
- Strong, proven sales skills.
- Experience of designing websites that increase sales significantly.
- A proven ability to revitalise brands that are flagging.

- Using statistical analysis to support arguments.
- Spotting trends in emerging buying habits and capitalising on them.

Identifying your unique combination

In Exercise 14, we identified your combination of talents. In Exercise 17 above, we identified your skills and experience. Now, we will use the results of these two exercises to identify your unique combination of talents, skills and experience to create your personal message. We are looking for the combination that makes you unique *in your environment*. Someone on the other side of the world may have the same combination as you but operate in a different context. Unless both of you do your business entirely electronically, you may not compete with each other directly.

Exercise 18
Your unique combination of talents, skills and experience

- -

Choose a talent, skill or type of experience that you feel is one of your strongest. Imagine you are in a circle with everyone in the world who has that particular talent, skill or experience. It may be hundreds, thousands or millions of people. It does not matter.

Now pick another of your talents, skills or experiences. Maybe lots of other people have that, too. You and they are in another big circle which overlaps with the first.

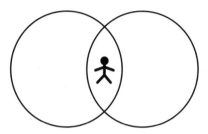

You and a relatively small number of people are in both circles.

Now pick a third talent, skill or experience that you and other people have. If we add a third circle to the diagram, you and an even smaller number of people will have all three talents, skills or experiences.

For example, the first circle might include everyone in the world who has a degree in engineering. The second circle might include everyone who speaks both French and English. The third circle might include everyone who has a talent for finding practical solutions to everyday problems.

Make a list of the three to six talents, skills or experiences that, taken together, make you rare, if not unique:

1 . . . .

2 . . . .

3 ....

4 ....

5 ....

6 ....

- -

Please note that not all the points listed in your unique combination have to be related to your work – it may be something else that makes you different.

Everything you say about yourself has to be objective and measurable. It is important not to make vague assertions such as 'I am a leader' or 'I am entrepreneurial'. This is where your 'hook' is particularly important as it encourages the listener to ask further questions.

For example, if you are a leader or an entrepreneur, it should be possible to say something measurable, such as:

- Successfully led teams of up to 20 expert consultants in my last three roles.

This hook encourages the listener to ask you more about the last three roles as well as the type of consultants that you led.

- Founded a retail business whose revenue grew to x million in five years and made a substantial profit of x amount.

In this hook, the listener is encouraged to ask you how you grew the revenue and also how you were able to make substantial profit.

It is best to avoid subjective descriptions such as 'a dynamic person'. Some people may think you are dynamic, others may disagree. Likewise, saying you are 'a good communicator' does not help much. Few people would say they were bad communicators!

Most people with a few years' work experience have a unique combination of talents, skills and experiences consisting of four to six points. You may be unique with only two or three.

Having built a full picture of yourself in Part 2, it is important to keep checking how your career is aligning with the understanding that you have developed your personal brand, and what aspects are most useful in the world of work. This helps you to define your direction and test your talents, skills and experience in relation to the real world. The more you check your skills and experience, it allows you to create a focus of where you want to work, how you want to work, and who you want to work with.

Now is a very good time to listen to the people who you have identified as helping you on this journey, to provide constructive criticism of your message. When we run seminars, we ask the participants to work in pairs. Each person drafts their unique combination and presents it to the other, who edits it. This greatly improves the end result.

It helps to do this exercise with someone who knows you well, or at least check the results with them afterwards. Having seen you in different situations, they can have useful insights. They may also realise that you have missed out something that you do naturally and take for granted. For example, you may do something purely for enjoyment which might, one day, become part of your job or business. Examples include photography, music, teaching and writing.

As we have already said, you should not market yourself as the cheapest. Anyone can offer to work for even less. It is better to base your unique combination on attributes that provide a real benefit to someone. If you build a brand that has significant value for other people, you can charge a higher price while retaining loyal customers.

Using your unique combination to market yourself

Once you know your unique combination of talents, skills and experience, you can use it in many ways. For example, you can use it in the Summary section on LinkedIn. It will help people to grasp what you have to offer and find ways of working with you.

Understanding your unique combination is particularly useful when you are looking for a new job, or new clients or customers.

It helps you to understand what you have to offer that makes you different. For example, if you are sending your CV to a hiring manager, it is often helpful if you summarise what you have to offer in four to six bullet points, which you can include in your introductory letter or email.

Many executive search firms, or firms of headhunters, use a technique known as an acid test, which summarises the criteria for a particular assignment in four to six bullet points. If several of the bullet points in your unique combination match those in the acid test, you may be put on the longlist right away, making it much more likely that you will end up on the shortlist and be offered the job.

If you are writing speculatively to an employer or hiring manager, you may not know their exact needs. However, by summarising what you have to offer, you will make it easier for them to choose you if an opportunity arises. You can write a short letter or email along the following lines so readers can see at a glance whether you have the skills and experience they need:

> '**I can offer you/your clients the following:**
>
> - **A 15-year track record in software, including 10 years in sales and marketing.**
> - **Experience of leading teams of up to 50 people, based in several countries.**
> - **Five years' experience as the chief executive of a high-growth company.**
> - **A working knowledge of Mandarin.'**

You can use your unique combination to extend your activities into new areas that employers, clients or customers will see as a logical progression. One of our examples did this at one point. They already had a reputation for solving problems within financial institutions. They then applied their knowledge of computers – which had previously been a hobby – to help a bank process information more efficiently. By combining this knowledge with their financial skills, they strengthened their reputation as a problem solver.

A woman working in public relations in the metallurgy sector found she was more excited about promoting individuals than companies. She therefore looked for a new role in which she could focus on what she did best. It was a challenge at first. Her network, including the headhunters she met, saw her as 'a corporate PR executive specialising in metallurgy' initially and not what she wanted to do.

Your brand often lags way behind what you do now, so it is essential to keep updating people. You may have broadened or deepened your activities, but most of your contacts are probably unaware that you have done so. You can start to expand your business by telling them what you do now, both face to face and online. One of the best ways is to give them concrete examples of work you have done recently. We will discuss this in Chapter 11 when we talk about telling your story.

Summarising what you do in a couple of sentences

Once you understand your unique combination of talents, skills and experience, you can express it even more concisely when you need to, particularly when someone asks, 'What do you do?'.

This is how one person answered the question: 'I analyse how people interact. Then I create IT solutions to help them overcome business problems quickly and efficiently.'

Another person said: 'I spot trends. Then I use numbers and practical examples to persuade clients to adopt new ideas that will make money for them.'

Some of us provide more than one service. We therefore need more than one version.

This is what one of the authors says (a) to companies: 'I help your people to fulfil their potential in ways that improve your bottom line'; and (b) to executives: 'I work with you to clarify what you want out of your future and help you achieve it.'

Summarising what you do in five seconds – your hook

Sometimes, you will need to be even more concise. Imagine you are at a social event. Someone asks what you do. Just when you have begun to answer, you are interrupted by someone who wants you to pass them a plate of food. Then the conversation moves on to another topic.

That person you were talking to could lead you to a great opportunity. It is best to assume that you have only a few seconds to tell them what you do. You therefore need a message that is concise and memorable. We call it a hook, as it encourages someone to ask a question. Your hook should be no longer than *five seconds*. If you say only that you are a headhunter, an accountant or a psychiatrist, the conversation may end there. If you mention two activities, at least twice as many people will want to know more. They will pick up on the topic that interests them most.

You can base your hook on your unique combination. That is, your hook incites others to probe further into your unique combination of skills and highlights what differentiates you from others. Here are some examples that explain why they are considered hooks. Each person has chosen two points from their unique combination:

- '**I'm a business psychologist with a marketing background.**' This works because people are often curious as to what a business psychologist is. When you couple this profession with marketing, people will be interested in exploring this link further by understanding how these two areas of expertise might complement each other.'

- '**I'm an investment banker specialising in mergers and acquisitions and a governor of a school for dyslexic children.**' This hook shows that this person's background in financial services is able to be applied and shared to help the school better govern its financial affairs. It provides the opportunity to, first, show that as an individual you use your expertise to help others in different areas of work and, second, it generates curiosity and conversation into the multiple dimensions through which you can offer your expertise.

- **'I'm an account director for an advertising agency. I also do a lot of photography.'**
  In this example, the hook shows how you can link your career with your hobbies, extending your unique value. The two work well together, because so much advertising is visual. Therefore, being a photographer can make you better at advertising, and vice versa.

- **'I'm studying journalism. At the moment, I'm getting some work experience with a local newspaper.'**
  This hook shows that your aspiration is to have a career in journalism and, to support this, you have been astute and acted proactively to get experience in the field so that you can better understand how journalism works, as well as providing you with credible experience when you go out into the job market.

- **'I'm an accountant. I focus on helping small businesses.'**
  This example helps clients to specifically understand what your area of service is. Many people either know someone who runs their own business or want to start one themselves and, therefore, as an accountant, they may approach you if you meet this need.

Your hook helps to communicate your unique combination and makes people remember you. For example, there are plenty of accountants, but few specialise in small businesses. That makes the person unique and memorable.

Exercise 19
Your five-second hook

- -

The aim is to catch people's attention and be memorable. Think of
two aspects of what you do that could interest other people and
are likely to make you unique. Write down one or two sentences,
in the style you would use during a casual conversation. Test your
three-second statement on friends and family members. Then test
it on people you meet for the first time. Make a mental note of what
gets their attention and leads to a longer conversation.

- -

One example's statement was: 'I'm a banker. I do lots of restructuring.' Another said: 'I'm in sales and marketing. I help companies to
grow faster.'

Having established your hook and gained feedback from others,
you will need to refine your goals, plans and tasks. The GROW
Model provides the vehicle that allows you to refine the choices you
wish to pursue and help you explain what you do.[1]

Using the GROW Model

When we get down to the question: 'What are we going to do?',
the GROW Model is useful to help us work out exactly the order of
actions required to get to our goal. This reflective tool will enable
you to explore the different routes to where you want to go to ensure
the best approach is taken.

There will always be obstacles in your way to any course of action
and a lot of 'yes . . . buts' – using the model you can check if the
'yes . . . buts' are simply based on coming away from the way you
normally operate that is unsettling you, or that the obstacle you face
needs a different route to overcome it to continue your 'new' journey.

The GROW Model stands for: Goal, Reality, Options/Obstacles and, lastly, Will/Way forward.

What do we want to achieve by the end of this meeting?

What is happening now? What resources do we have/need?

Goal **Reality**

GROW

Will **Options**

What can we commit to, who will do it and by when?

What ideas can we come up with to achieve our goal?

The GROW Model

Source: Carol Wilson, The Grow Model, Culture at Work, Retrieved from https://www.coachingcultureatwork.com/the-grow-model/

The questions to ask are:

1 Goal – Where am I going?

Here it is useful to clarify your goal from a SMART point of view:

- *Specific* – What you want to achieve.
- *Measurable* – Can you identify progress, can it be broken down into smaller tasks to motivate you to do the next?
- *Achievable* – Can it be accomplished? Are there other ways?
- *Relevant* – Is it worth achieving? Is it the right time?
- *Time bound* – Normally, a task takes as long as the time you give to it. Too soon and you will be disappointed by lack of progress, and too long will mean your motivation may wane. Also, we need to be conscious that we normally believe we can achieve something in less time than is feasible.

2 **Reality** – Where are you now? What is your present position? Are you on the journey or about to start? What support do you need from others? Have you got examples from your past that help you to feel you will be able to attain your goal?

3 **Options and obstacles** – What options do you have? What else could you do? What are the pros and cons of the options? What is getting in the way of choosing particular options? What are the side effects of choosing particular options?

4 **Will and the way forward** – What is your motivation for particular options? Do you have a strong desire to take a particular one? Who can help you to achieve your goal?

You can start working with the GROW Model based on the information above. Important points are: ask yourself the questions people may ask of you, explore the reality and your options in the real world, draw up an action plan and follow up on identifying where your brand can have the most impact in the world of work.

Key takeaways

- When we start to look at the world of work and what interests us, we need to start applying what we have learned about ourselves to the real world.

- We need to add our skills and experience to our unique combination of talents and use the result to market ourselves effectively.

- It is important to convey our message about who we are and what we do in a succinct personal message lasting no longer than five seconds.

- We need to ensure our message has 'hooks' to entice the listener to ask for more information.

- Using the GROW Model, we can apply what we know about ourselves to the real world to clarify our course of action.

Note

1 Whitmore, J. (2017) *Coaching for Performance*, Performance Consultants International, 5th Edition, Nicholas Brealey Publishing.

chapter 11

Storytelling

You have articulated your hook, tested it with others and then worked through the GROW Model. Now, you will be better able to write stories that support what you do. Once someone shows interest in what you do, you will need to tell stories about yourself that amplify how you add value in the real world.

Storytelling is an important tool in your ability to influence others. It enables you to create a deeper connection with an audience by adding the human aspect to what you have done, helping your audience to see how *you* operate with the skills and experiences many others may have, that set you apart.

Hiring managers are certainly looking for the technical skills and experience but they are also looking for the 'people' skills and experience as well. You also need to be aware of the other person and the context within which they work so that you can choose a story that resonates with them.

As a recent *Harvard Business Review* article states:

'Like all great stories, the experiences you talk about will need clear context to resonate with your listeners. Storytelling experts call context the "why" that drives the plot of a narrative. It gives your audience a reason to listen through to the end and arrive happily at your resolution.'[1]

Stories transmit both knowledge and meaning and enable you to drive a deeper connection with your audience and elevate the meaning of your brand into their lives.

A powerful way to make you visible

Rob Biesenbach, a former vice-president of a top 10 public relations firm, says:

'Whether you're selling, interviewing, or just representing yourself in the marketplace, offer people something they can't refuse: a specific story that lends power to your words.'

He goes on to say that stories are the most powerful way to get more of what you want out of your career and your life.[2]

Robin Dunbar, anthropologist and evolutionary psychologist, estimates that around two-thirds of our conversations are about who is doing what and with whom. In other words: stories.

Storytelling is second nature to us all. If we develop our innate ability to tell stories, we can do so clearly, authentically and effectively.

Most people use facts, figures and rational arguments to try and convince others. They rarely succeed. But stories can convey emotions effectively and bring energy to our communication. We remember what we feel. And it's our emotions that inspire us to take action, not facts.

Stories spark our interest and transport our imaginations to places where we can visualise the events being recounted.

Stories also help prevent what psychologists call 'confirmation bias' – the tendency to favour information that confirms our preconceptions, regardless of whether that information is true. Confirmation bias causes people to gather evidence and recall information from memory selectively, and then interpret it in a way that suits them. So, if someone tries to convince us to change our minds with facts and figures, we often dig our heels in and resist.

Confirmation bias occurs in change-management initiatives, sales situations and financial decisions, for example. Our personal beliefs are also subject to confirmation bias. However, if you tell a story, it will gently guide the listener to your conclusions, without provoking them with opposing facts.

If you think about it, great leaders are also great storytellers. For instance, when you hear the names Steve Jobs and Oprah Winfrey you can instantly recall their stories that describe how their earlier life experiences have shaped who they are as leaders and what drove them towards achieving their ambitions.

So, bring your communication to life and make it memorable by using a story to make your point. You can then back it up with appropriate facts and figures.

It is crucially important to be honest and truthful in those stories as, often, people overinflate their impact and it is something hiring managers are good at uncovering and, once uncovered, trust disappears and the hiring manager becomes wary about anything you say. Authenticity is the key. If you are hiding anything, your manner and confidence level will probably show something is not right when speaking about yourself to others.

Facts tell, stories sell

Most of us find it easier to remember a story than a series of facts. We tell stories about people as a way of illustrating their character or abilities. You can also tell a story about yourself that illustrates your talents, skills and/or experience, in an authentic way.

Most finance directors in the UK are accountants in dark suits, aged between 30 and 60. Since every business above a certain size usually has a finance director, there are thousands of people who fit this description. If you asked them whether they were good communicators, practically all of them would say yes. This makes it difficult for a finance director to stand out from the crowd.

On one occasion, we interviewed a finance director whose mother tongue was Cantonese. The candidate mentioned that he had attended an awards ceremony in London where he had interpreted for Jackie Chan, the star of many martial-arts films. This anecdote works very well from a branding point of view. In a sentence or two, it tells us that (a) he is bilingual/bicultural, (b) he is probably comfortable in front of a large audience and (c) he has connections that extend beyond finance. But, above all, it makes him *memorable*. We remember him as the' Jackie Chan guy'.

When you pass on stories about yourself, the facts must stand up to scrutiny. Some hiring managers have met several people who claim to have launched the same consumer product or to have completed the same financial transaction. They cannot all be telling the truth. It is more credible to say you were a member of the team that worked on a particular project and what your role was in that project. What is important is to be specific about your contribution.

The aim is to explain both *what* your contribution was and *how* you approached the project. What you do not want is for an experienced interviewer to ask questions that will show that you are not telling the truth. It is also important to give credit to your team for what they achieved, with your guidance.

For example: building a significant engineering structure. *What* is your specific role in the building of the structure and the *how* explains how you related with stakeholders such as the planners, architects, engineers, etc. That is, 'I was responsible for working with the engineers to ensure that the engineering aspects of the project met all key milestones. The engineering aspect of the project was completed within the three-year time frame.'

Although many people enjoy hearing stories, they still want straight answers to their questions. If someone asks, 'Can you do X?', it is best to say yes or no and support your statement with an example. If you avoid giving straight answers, people may feel that you are hiding something. Better still is to tell a story about your experience in 'X' which clarifies your skills and experience. Using the same example above, if asked the question, 'were you the primary project manager on this engineering project?', you can honestly say, 'No', but you can explain what you did was to coordinate and work with experts to achieve a successful engineering build. For example, 'I met weekly with the engineers to run through all key and upcoming milestones and address any concerns or potential hiccups that might happen'. Decisions were made and problems articulated and solved in a timely fashion.

It usually helps to mention other projects, preferably recent ones, where you can show that there is consistence in the way you work and what you do.

What to say when you're looking for work

If you have no work right now, it is important to be positive while making it clear that you are looking for a new opportunity. Here are some examples of an opening statement:

- 'I finished at XYZ Co. a month ago. I'm now looking for another full-time role in marketing. In the meantime, I'm helping a friend to launch a new product.'

- 'I learned my trade as a financial controller at ABC Hotels. I'm now looking for new opportunities in property and manufacturing.'

- 'I was a software developer at FGH until recently. There's a short-age of IT people with my specific skills at the moment, so I've been looking at several really interesting opportunities.'

The last statement is a good one as it leads the listener to ask about your 'specific skills'. If you talk only in generalities, when it comes to others making decisions about hiring you, you will not stand out and fall into the list of mediocre candidates.

It is also better not to talk about why you left your old company unless the question comes up. In case it does, it is worth preparing an honest answer that shows you have moved on with a positive attitude. For example:

- 'Last year, the overheads doubled just before the revenues halved. Half the staff had to leave, including me, so I'm now looking for another opportunity.'
- 'After the merger, our whole department relocated to Geneva. I couldn't move my family, so I'm now looking for a similar role in this area.'

It is best to keep it brief. We have often seen candidates who are still upset with their previous company and show it. The more you talk about negative points in your past career, the less attractive you will be to new employers, who are interested in what you can do for them *now*. However, at some point, you may be asked to summarise your career. You must be clear about who you are and what you want to do. For example:

- 'I've spent most of my career in property, most recently as a business development manager for North America. I now believe I have the ability to extend my skills in a global role.'
- 'I've managed departments in several manufacturing industries and have led change programmes which I really enjoyed. Now I'm planning to explore management consultancy roles.'

It is best to be specific, but not prescriptive, about what you are looking for. The person you are talking to may think of someone you should meet and tell you right away. Equally, they may bump into someone who might be able to help you a few days later and then get back in touch with you.

Evoking archetypes

We know from the world of marketing that evoking archetypes adds substance to your brand. How you use your archetypes is through language that evokes them and allows others to recognise them. Stories that you have identified as useful to project your brand can be enhanced by using these metaphors relating to your archetypes. For example, one of the authors' archetypes is the Jester. A story that would reflect this metaphor is that they often work with leaders to provoke, disrupt and transform their organisations, by speaking 'truth to power'. In thought-provoking workshops, the author creates a safe space so that leaders can engage in uncomfortable conversations and they nudge them towards making behavioural change and shifting mindset.

By now, you would have identified one or two archetypes that align with your purpose, values and talents. It is important that you retain your brand authenticity by ensuring that you do not overuse metaphors so that your brand is not diluted.

For example, as a business psychologist, one of the authors usually evokes the Magician – they help people to transform their careers. However, they often start off by evoking the Caregiver, so people feel comfortable and realise they can trust them.

If we now refer to some of the other archetypes, we can see how evoking them would be bad for their brand:

- The Innocent: too ethereal, e.g. a client wants help in dealing with reality.

- The Jester: sometimes too flippant or blunt, e.g. a client may expect the author to take their problem and help them solve it.

- The Outlaw: too risky, e.g. the client does not want a psychologist who breaks the rules.

- The Ruler: too controlling, e.g. the client may prefer the freedom to find their own way.

Choosing the right metaphor

Spanish philosopher José Ortega y Gasset said:

'The metaphor is perhaps one of man's most fruitful potentialities. Its efficacy verges on magic.'

Many of us use metaphors every day. They affect how we think about the world – and behave – in subtle ways. For example, many people say, 'Time is money.' They talk about 'borrowed time' and 'time running out'. They perceive time as both valuable and limited.

Metaphors can be equally powerful in expressing and strengthening your brand. People often do this unconsciously when they are being authentic. However, metaphors may work for or against you and your brand.

One example is military metaphors, which rest on the notion that 'work is war'. This Ruler archetype can be useful when you are talking about launching a marketing campaign or capturing a share of the market, but be careful that the metaphor relates to the organisation you are potentially working for. A charity, for instance, may find such a metaphor inappropriate!

If you were a chief executive talking to shareholders, you might say, 'We will wipe out the competition' or 'Our marketing plan will capture X per cent of the market'. This can work well if everything else you say and do evokes the Ruler. However, it can clash badly with other archetypes such as the Caregiver. So, for example, imagine that you are the chief executive of a chain of private healthcare clinics and you promise to wipe out the competition. In this case, the Ruler vocabulary clashes with the Caregiver archetype. Metaphors work only if the archetype they evoke is consistent with the brand you are building and the context within which you are working.

A danger of metaphors is that they can descend into clichés, particularly in written material. This makes you look unimaginative. We know one consultancy firm whose website exhorted readers to 'Think outside the box!' They wanted to evoke the Creator archetype. However, the way it did so was unoriginal and actually demonstrated a lack of creativity.

Metaphors work best if used sparingly. Once you know your preferred archetype, you can experiment with metaphors that are consistent with it. When talking to an individual or a small group, you can choose a metaphor that will work with them. If you were saving a company from disaster and wished to evoke the Hero, for example, you might tell the staff and shareholders that the company was 'fighting for survival'. This could inspire them to support you.

In a more stable situation, you might evoke the Ruler. You could say you were 'strengthening the foundations', thereby encouraging people to place their trust in you. If you were evoking the Creator, you could say you were 'building a platform for growth' or 'bringing forth new talent in the business'. That would help to attract people who wanted to be part of something new and exciting.

Exercise 20
Metaphors to strengthen your brand

- -

Think about the archetype that best relates to what you do. Which metaphors would reinforce your brand identity? Which would help you to extend your brand?

- -

Another example of a person who believed they evoked the Creator archetype decided that artistic metaphors worked best for them. This is what they said about the process: 'I work towards a consensus by asking people to imagine a picture of the way they want their organisation to be. Then I ask them which elements are missing from the picture. Just like any artist, I am applying information in layers like an oil painting until the picture starts to feel right. Often the parts come together and people come up with potential highlights which add to the richness of the picture. I usually start with an outline of what I want to achieve and that helps me to identify the parts of the picture I need to spend more time on.'

Yet another example is of a person who loves architecture, so they find it an easy metaphor to use in their work. They believe they evoke both the Jester and the Hero:

'I build relationships the way well-known architects build eye-catching buildings: standing out from the crowd, pushing back the boundaries, taking risks. People remember me because I'm not afraid to speak out for what I believe needs to happen. I build some strong foundations with stakeholders before I present radical ideas. I get existing clients to mention me. I structure what I'm going to say, based firmly on the brief, but I remain true to myself and I'm never afraid to disagree.'

Using words that evoke your archetype

By choosing your words carefully, you can evoke your main archetype and strengthen your brand identity. Here are the 12 archetypes, with words you can use to evoke them.

The Caregiver

Caring. Altruism. Help. Protect. Comfort. Nurture. Support. Affection. Empathy. Commitment. Friendly. Concern.

The Creator

Create. Innovate. Self-expression. Non-conformist. Vision. Invent. Inspiration. Daydream. Fantasy. Experiment. Unconventional. Aesthetic.

The Explorer

Discover. Seek. Wander. Find out. Adventure. Pioneer. Freedom. Risk. Fearless. Curious. Experience. Restless.

The Hero

Courage. Prove your worth. Challenge. Compete. Strong. Powerful. Determination. Persevere. Prevail. Rescue. Discipline. Character. Warrior. Turnaround.

The Innocent

Purity. Goodness. Happiness. Simplicity. Moral. Trusting. Honest. Authentic. Perfectionist. Stress-reducing. Romantic. Mystic.

The Jester

Live for the moment. Break the rules. Impulsive. Challenge. Prank. Provoke. Entertain. Mischievous. Manipulate. Playful. Seeker of truth. Outrageous. Clever.

The Lover

Partner. Harmony. Pleasure. Intimacy. Togetherness. Beautiful. Romance. Relationship. Attractive. Passion. Collaborate. Gratitude. Appreciation. Commitment. Friendship.

The Magician

Vision. Transform. Change. Spiritual. Mediate. Finds win–win solutions. Makes dreams come true. Synchronicity. Meaningful coincidences. Charisma. The experience of flow. Miracles.

The Ordinary Person

Connect. Belong. Friendship. Down-to-earth. Functional. Straightforward. Wholesome. Realist. Team spirit. Unpretentious.

The Outlaw

Break the rules. Revolution. Rebel. Disrupt. Destroy. Outrageous. Radical. Counter-culture. Unconventional. Outsider. Independent thinking.

The Ruler

Control. Order. Commanding. Authority. Power. Substance. Impressive. Organise. Responsible. Manager. Administrate. Dominate.

The Sage

Scholar. Knowledge. Wisdom. Truth. Objectivity. Expert. Advise. Mentor. Teach. Research. Detect. Think. Interpret. Understand.

Key takeaways

- Storytelling is a powerful way to get messages across to an audience.
- Storytelling enables you to connect more to your audience by combining technical skills and experience with people skills and experience.
- Use metaphors to evoke your archetype that support the telling of powerful stories.
- Use Stories to explain your experience to be remembered.

Notes

1 Kurnoff, J. and Lazarus, L. (2021) 'The key to landing your next job? Storytelling', *Harvard Business Review*.

2 Biesenbach, R. (2018) *Unleash the Power of Storytelling: Win Hearts, Change Minds, Get Results*, Eastlawn Media.

3 Landau, M. J. et al (Ed) (2014) *The Power of Metaphor*, American Psychological Association.

chapter 12

Presence

Some people have a strong presence. You can feel it when you are with them. These people establish a rapport with you and they consistently attract colleagues, clients, customers, investors and/or fans. This personal magnetism is often described as *charisma*. It is a valuable aspect of a strong personal brand.

All the work you have done so far contributes to your presence – as the more aware you are of yourself and the more you allow others to see your authentic self, including your purpose, values and talents, the more others will see and remember your presence.

It is something you cannot fake. It has to come from within.

We believe there are three main ways in which you can develop even more presence. This chapter will show you how.

What is presence?

One aspect of presence is connection: giving people your complete attention – literally being present. You are with them in the here and now – not in the past or the future, or in some other place. Many successful business people, entertainers and politicians are good at being present. If someone is present *with you*, they give their full attention to what you are saying and doing, and what you may be thinking and feeling. Their presence enables them to connect with everyone they meet.

We can also understand presence when we experience a lack of it. Some people are not present when they communicate. If you watch people during a meeting, you can see that some are not present at all. For instance, words come out of their mouths, but they do not match these with their body language. Or, their eyes may constantly dart around, or their attention is diverted elsewhere, often on their mobile phones.

We all have distracting thoughts, particularly if there's a lot on your mind. You may not be actively listening if you find yourself thinking about how you are going to respond, or about a different viewpoint, or, even what you might be having for lunch. All this gets in the way of communication. It is not enough for you to listen. The other person needs to *feel* listened to. They can tell if you are giving them your full attention and if you are present. If you do listen and pay attention, you can build a strong rapport with them.

The following exercise will help you to calm your mind and be present.

Exercise 21
Being present

- -

This exercise will take you 5–10 minutes. It is important to sit upright during this exercise – if you lie down, you may fall asleep. It is best if someone reads it out while you close your eyes and listen.

Alternatively, you can record it and play it back. Whoever reads it out should leave big pauses between each paragraph.

Sit upright on your chair. Keep your feet flat on the floor and as far apart as your hips. Keep your hands open in front of you and rest them on your thighs. Close your eyes. Allow your body to relax, letting go of any tension.

Feel where you are now: the clothes touching your skin, the weight of your body on the chair, the air on your face and hands.

Become aware of taste and smell. Listen, as far as possible, into the distance, beyond the sounds nearby.

Listen carefully for a while.

Let go of any thoughts or judgements about the sounds. Rest your attention on the breath as it flows in and out of your body. Do not try to change any of this. Simply allow your attention to rest only upon your breath.

Every now and then, your attention will wander. When it does, do not judge yourself. Simply bring your attention gently back to the breath.

Open your eyes. Notice the colour and form of the objects around you. Feel the weight of your body on the chair, the air on your face and hands. Remain aware of this for a while.

Most people have to do this exercise several times before it has a major effect. It helps you develop a *quiet mind*. As it says in the Chinese classic *Tao Te Ching*: 'Empty yourself of everything. Let the mind become still.' Although it takes effort, it brings many benefits. One of them is a stronger rapport with other people. The more carefully you listen to them, the more information you will absorb and the better they will feel about you.

Once you have practised this exercise a few times on your own, you can use aspects of it when you are with other people. For example, when you are listening to someone speak, you can feel the breath flowing in and out of your body at the same time. This helps to prevent your attention from wandering off elsewhere. Another example is when you are standing on a stage, speaking to a large audience. Every now and then, you can pause and feel the sensations throughout your body, or the weight of your body on the floor. It will help to ensure that you remain present with your audience and are not carried away by what you are saying.

Technology can disrupt your rapport with other people, if you allow it. If you leave your mobile phone switched on, or keep looking at a computer screen, you cannot give someone your full attention. One solution is to take out your mobile and say, 'I'm going to switch this off now.' You then do so and remove your mobile from sight. Many people will follow your example.

Acceptance

Some people's presence comes from *acceptance*. They accept themselves as they are and the situation as it is. They also accept other people.

You can feel when someone accepts themselves. They are at peace and do not pretend to be anything they're not. They do not judge themselves or other people. They accept you exactly as you are. Sometimes, you can sense it in their body language and their smile, and in the way they treat you. Acceptance is an aspect of love – it draws people to you.

If you accept things as they are, rather than as you think they should be, then you can make appropriate plans and take action. As Deepak Chopra says: 'Accept the present, intend the future.'

Here is an exercise to help you with acceptance.

Exercise 22
Acceptance

Before you get out of bed, say to yourself: 'Today I shall accept everything that occurs.' As you go about your daily activities, keep tethering yourself to the present moment. This will help you to observe what is going on around you. Notice the way people speak and behave, the weather, the pace at which things happen or don't happen. Notice the thoughts that appear in your mind. Say to yourself: 'I accept everything that occurs.'

If you remain in the present, you can also observe any judgements as they appear in your mind: 'She shouldn't have said that', 'People shouldn't do that', 'What a stupid situation', and so on. However, instead of clinging to these judgements, you can let them go. Don't try to resist them. You can just let them go.

Imagine you are standing on a bridge, looking down into a river as it rushes past. All kinds of thoughts, including judgements, are carried along down the river, while you observe them. Fairly soon, they will vanish. New ones may appear. You can let go of them, too. Say to yourself: 'I accept everything that occurs.'

You still *care* about what goes on around you. If you remain in the present, you can take the right action at the right time. If a child or a dog runs out into the road, you can intervene immediately. However, whether observing or taking action, you avoid judging. It frees you from negative emotions that sap your energy. It helps you do what needs to be done, at just the right time.

Once you have taken the necessary action, you can relax. Place your attention on the breath flowing in and out, and on the sensations throughout your body. Return to the present moment. Remind yourself, 'I accept everything that occurs.'

- -

Presence is not easy to pin down. However, we know it when we see it or feel it in someone else. If you (i) remain in the present and (ii) accept yourself and others, you will develop a stronger presence of your own.

Pursuing your purpose and mission

Pursuing your purpose and mission involves applying the talents you love to use, in a way that is consistent with your values, to an activity that absorbs you. If you are present in any meeting, you will be aware of both your purpose and mission. By pursuing both, people are more likely to be attracted by the energy you exude when you do what you love. Some will be attracted by your talent(s), particularly if they have a similar talent but have not fully applied it yet. For example, some people have a talent for leadership, but have yet to realise it.

Tribes is a thought-provoking book written by marketing guru Seth Godin, who says: 'Leadership . . . is about creating change that you believe in . . . Through your actions as a leader, you attract a tribe that wants to follow you. The tribe has a worldview that matches the message you're sending . . . I think most people have it upside down. Being charismatic doesn't make you a leader. Being a leader makes you charismatic.'[1]

As we said in Chapter 1, if you are true to your talents and your values, you will be *authentic*. While some people with opposing values will keep their distance from you, you will also attract people who share some of your values and appreciate what you do best. It is much easier to work with people who are on the same wavelength. It is also far more productive and enjoyable.

When we look at the above exercises, we also realise that our presence comes from the clarity we have about ourselves that others can also see.

The more we know about ourselves, an aura of both confidence and credibility develops, based on the way we operate, that underpins our presence.

Key takeaways

- Presence and being present in all our dealings with others is fundamental to our personal brand.
- It is something that cannot be faked.
- It underpins our authenticity.

Note

1 Godin, S. (2008) *Tribes: We Need You to Lead Us*, Piatkus Books.

chapter 13

Building your brand offline

Once you know who you are and where you are going, it is time to become more visible. In this chapter, we will describe ways of putting yourself on the map offline – essentially, how you can maximise your brand so that you become more visible in your market. It's all about how you stand out!

Combining what you have learnt about yourself so far with the following steps can help to position yourself so that you stand out.

Understanding the impact of your brand in society

Until now, we have taken you on a journey where you have examined who you are on the 'inside' and how this relates and translates through your personal brand. Now, it is time to look at how you present on the 'outside'. In other words, an 'outside-in' as opposed to 'inside-out' insight to your brand.

In Part 2, identifying your purpose, values and talent helped you to focus on who you are, what you stand for and your unique set of skills and capabilities. At the beginning of Part 3, explaining what you do, your stories and presence enabled you to bring together these elements to cohesively package your personal brand.

Building your brand visibly involves checking out what you have learnt about yourself, and how you add value, with what the outside world needs and wants now. The question is: how do I position myself so that I best stand out against other candidates or competitors?

As the world has changed regarding how people develop their careers, the process of securing and maintaining visibility has become increasingly complex. For example, our careers can see us moving locally, nationally or internationally. We can switch roles, switch sectors, return to work after a significant absence, switch between self-employment and inhouse roles, etc. So, these differing elements have to be considered. Where would you like to move and what areas would you like to move into while, at the same time, being cognisant of your own capabilities and what makes you stand out.

How do your stories and presence align with this next step? What are you telling the world about yourself? Have you identified what you would like to do?

Here, we offer ways to help you develop your offline presence, making you better placed to promote your brand.

Speaking engagements

One of the best ways to reach more people is to speak to them in groups. It could be at a bespoke event with two or three colleagues or clients who you have personally invited, it might be 10 people at a round-table event, or hundreds at a large venue where you are the keynote speaker.

Good things tend to happen whenever you stand up and say something useful to a large audience. Someone might want to discuss a job or consulting project with you or invite you to speak at another venue. Being a speaker gives you credibility on which you can build. The stronger your brand, the more likely you are to be invited to be a keynote speaker.

We appreciate that public speaking can be emotive. For instance, you may be afraid of public speaking. Many people are terrified. They worry about what the audience will think or say about them. Some people in the audience may also be afraid – afraid that you will talk for hours, make weak jokes or endlessly promote your business.

You can overcome this, first by changing what you focus on. Unless you are a professional entertainer, you have probably been invited to speak because you know something that could help the audience. All you have to do is *focus* on helping them. If you focus on one thing, it shifts your attention away from everything else, including any unhelpful thoughts. Instead of being self-conscious, you will literally forget yourself.

Once people realise you are making a sincere effort to help them, they usually relax and are more receptive. Even if you are talking about your own experiences, you can focus on how these will help your audience. Most of them will be there to learn from your talk.

It may also be useful to think of a time when you were passionate about a topic and you used your voice to evoke this passion. You might remember that speaking came very easily to you. Through the exercises that you previously completed in this book, you will be able to see clearly how and when you were at your most passionate and, therefore, will be more able to awaken the voice within that overcame your fears. The more you know about yourself, the more you will utilise the strength within you to speak to an audience.

Beyond this, public speaking is a question of preparation and practice. The more thoroughly you prepare and the more often you speak, the better you will become.

Getting to know your audience

A fundamental practice of public speaking is getting to know your audience. You may already know your audience well. If not, there are ways to break down barriers, build rapport and empathise with the audience's wants and needs. Being a good public speaker is about addressing what your listeners want and need to hear and not what you want to say. Put their agenda ahead of yours and demonstrate self-awareness, empathy and foresight.

Demonstrating foresight is possible by finding out about your audience before you speak – get to know what is in their heads and hearts. Talk to the organiser a few days beforehand to find out what might motivate your audience. Ask about the audience members' backgrounds, what they want from your talk, what they like and do not like, and what depth of knowledge they already have, so that you know how to meet them where they are. If possible, prior to the event, meet with a few key members of the audience to understand what information is useful for them. What gets them out of bed in the morning or keeps them awake at night? What is their reality? Of equal importance is gaining insight to their nationalities and cultural backgrounds. If you are going to speak to them in a language other than their mother tongue, think of ways to simplify your language.

Demonstrating self-awareness is about being aware of the concept of 'emotional contagion'. That is, what you emote is contagious and can infect others, for better or for worse. So, if you are anxious, this will come through and the audience will share your anxiety; if you are passionate, this will shine through and your audience will share your sense of excitement. Always do your best to manage your emotions before being with them and be aware of what functions your emotions serve.

On the day, if you arrive at the venue early, you can chat with members of the audience. Those who get there first are usually keen to hear what you have to say. If you talk to them and find out their names, you will already have a few supporters when you stand up and speak. They are more likely to ask good questions and contribute to the discussion at the end of your talk.

Moving around also helps you connect with your audience. Some speakers appear rooted to the spot, twisting their necks so they can read words off the screen behind them. It is better to walk out from behind the desk or lectern and engage with your audience, looking at the screen now and then. If you are talking to a small group, or have a radio microphone, you can walk among them, which is even better. Some talk show hosts do this to great effect.

Addressing one person at a time

If you are speaking to a large audience, you may find yourself staring into space, particularly if you are dazzled by floodlights and your eyes have not adjusted. It helps to focus on one sympathetic person at a time and talk to them. To begin with, you may have to focus on someone you can barely see. They and the people around them will usually pay more attention, because they will feel involved. Once you have spoken to them for a few seconds, pick another person in a different part of the room. That way, different groups will be drawn in. Make sure you include someone in the back row and someone on either side of you, so everyone feels involved.

Some television presenters use a simple technique. Although millions of people may be watching, they think of one friend or family member. Then they look into the lens and talk to that person. It helps the presenter to remain relaxed and confident. What is key is preparation and practice. Even if your engagement is for only 10 minutes, prepare thoroughly so that you feel grounded and can anticipate and respond to any questions or eventualities that might arise.

Structuring your material coherently

Your talk will be much easier to deliver if you structure it well. Then you can relax, put your message across and answer questions. Listeners will grasp your argument and remember more of what you have said. You can do all of this using the *Pyramid Principle* developed by Barbara Minto. At the top of the pyramid, your presentation should convey the main message. For example, 'Building your brand will transform your career'. This message can be broken down into a series of statements, the first of which is 'You already have a brand'. This becomes the heading on the first slide, or whatever presentation tool you choose. You can then break down this statement into a series of points – usually between two and four. If you use PowerPoint or a similar tool, applying the pyramid principle will help you. When we give talks on *Brand You*, our first slide often looks like the one below.

You already have a brand

- 'Your brand is what people say about you when you are not in the room.' Jeff Bezos, founder of Amazon.
- It's not just who you know, it's who knows you.
- Most people do not manage their brands. You can.

Some people memorise a speech to accompany their slides. This is a daunting task and usually makes them sound wooden. Equally, you should avoid reading the text word for word, which is boring and causes 'death by PowerPoint'. It is better to use prompts, so you talk about one point at a time. You can add examples and anecdotes as they occur to you.

If you have met some members of your audience, you can include examples that are relevant to them. You will then speak naturally, as you would during a conversation. If possible, allow people to ask brief questions as you go along. They will pay closer attention and learn more. If you relax and enjoy it, your audience will feel good about you and your message.

Humour breaks down barriers and keeps people interested. Some speakers tell set-piece jokes, but that has its risks. People may have heard the joke before. They may not share your sense of humour, particularly if they are from a different culture. For us, it feels more natural to make light-hearted remarks, dependent on the situation, as we go along. It is certainly less risky. In some countries, such as Britain, there is a tradition of self-deprecating humour – making remarks at your own expense. Elsewhere, this is not common practice. However, you can still have fun. Your audience would prefer to be entertained as well as informed.

An ideal format is a presentation consisting of 10 slides, each of which communicates one point, supported by a series of sub-points. If you allow 2–3 minutes per slide, 10 pages of PowerPoint will give you a presentation lasting 20–30 minutes, just the length of time many people can concentrate without a break. They will be grateful if you keep it brief. That also leaves plenty of time for questions and/ or exercises.

Once you have given your talk, it is good practice to post your slides on your host's website. That way, people who were unable to attend can still get the gist of what you said. You can also put your presentation on a website such as SlideShare (www.slideshare.net), and promote it via Twitter, Facebook, LinkedIn, etc.

Some hosts like to record talks by visiting speakers, which you can then promote in a similar way. However, if you are using material from a book or course you have written, be careful about copyright. It can be difficult to package and sell audio material if you have already provided something similar for free.

Once you get used to it, public speaking is no big deal. It is just another way to send your message out into the world. If it is something you really believe in – and you focus on serving your audience – then you will be authentic and find it much easier to overcome any fear of presenting.

Your main archetype that you identified in Chapter 9 should come across in your presentation, through your material, the metaphors you use, and the way you deliver it. For example, if you are a safety expert giving a talk on how to avoid accidents at work, you may evoke the Caregiver. If you are a stand-up comedian telling people about embarrassing moments in your life, you may evoke the Jester and/or the Ordinary Person. If you are naturally outrageous, you may evoke the Outlaw.

Television and radio

The audiences for both television and radio have become highly fragmented. Before spending time on a television or radio appearance it is worth checking how many people normally tune in and what their backgrounds are.

If you are being interviewed, it is essential to be well informed and confident. You should also check why you are being interviewed. Particularly in these times of social media, be careful about what you say, as you may be quoted out of context. On one occasion, one of the authors was contacted by a national television station that wanted him to talk about the effects of an industrial dispute. Three hours later, a presenter and cameraman came to their house and interviewed them for an hour. The following day, the news broke and the interview was reduced to a 15-second sound bite taken completely out of context.

Being quoted in newspapers and magazines

One of the quickest ways to become visible is to be quoted in the press. Articles (and photos) can remain visible on the internet for years. If you become an expert in your field, journalists will probably approach you at some point.

It is best to avoid giving opinions on other people or contentious situations. Quite apart from the legal risks, negative remarks reflect badly on you, the commentator. If an article says you 'declined to comment', it still helps to build your brand. The fact that you were mentioned shows you are an authority. Declining to comment helps to build your reputation for discretion and professionalism.

If you are a reliable and accurate source, some journalists will keep coming back and may be interested in further material from you. It is a good idea to follow them on social media, so you can stay connected with them. Journalists work to tight deadlines, so they rely on key contacts for an opinion or a quotation that helps to build their story. Many local newspapers and specialist magazines have a small staff and are short of interesting copy. You may find that they publish your article or press release verbatim. However, if you attempt to force-feed a story to journalists, particularly those in the national press, it can backfire. It is much better to treat them with respect and build a reputation as a reliable source of information.

Writing a letter, article or book

If you enjoy writing and are good at it, an article for a newspaper or magazine can help to build your profile. Writing a letter to the editor is even easier, especially if you do so by email. If you read previous letters to the editor you will see the kind of material that gets published and can tailor yours accordingly.

It is best to say something constructive that other readers will find interesting, rather than simply attacking another person's point of view. This is not to say that you cannot disagree with viewpoints already offered. You can simply state that you are offering another point of view from an alternative perspective.

If you are writing an article for established newspapers, magazines or journals, ensure that your material is evidence-based. That evidence does not have to be scientific research. It can simply be your experience. (If you have a theory, it is best to present it as such. That theory can then be tested by you or someone else.)

Writing a book requires a lot of effort, but can work wonders for your brand. To begin with, it may strengthen your existing relationships. If anyone has read your book, they are likely to think of you next time they have a need your expertise can fulfil. Books can also have a big impact on people you have never met. Most people keep books longer than other material and/or pass them on to friends and colleagues. If your book is published commercially by a third party, it helps to confirm that you are an expert.

Writing a high-quality book that will be read by lots of people takes time and effort. You can conserve energy by finding out what publishers want and writing a synopsis and sample chapter first, in the format they require. One way to do this is to work with an agent, who will help to shape and sell your book in return for a percentage of any advance and/or royalties. However, finding an agent who is willing to represent a first-time author is not always easy. It may be worth starting by attending a class or workshop for new authors run by your local writers' club. Examples include The London Writers' Club (www.londonwritersclub.com) and The California Writers Club (www.calwriters.org). These events will enable you to meet other writers, both published and aspiring, as well as agents, publishers and publicists.

If you are writing purely for existing and potential clients, you may decide to self-publish initially. This is simple and inexpensive. You can either use a print-on-demand service or approach a book designer and a digital printer directly. Either way, you can produce a few hundred copies, which you either sell or give away. It is also worth using a professional editor to make sure the final version is clear, logical and grammatically correct. This will help you to win more business.

An even cheaper option is to publish your book as an ebook initially. The costs of doing so are falling steadily.

If you are an expert in your field, you may wish to write a 'how to' book. If so, it is best to address a specific problem. This will help to make it a must-have for your readers, rather than a nice-to-have. A good example is *Getting to Yes*, the classic text on negotiation that has sold millions of copies in dozens of languages.

It is worth visiting a large bookshop to get an idea of what has already been written on the subject. The shop assistant may know of any bestsellers. You can also ask potential readers if they have read anything similar. Did they like it? Would they recommend it to a friend? Once you find a book on the subject you have in mind, flick through it and look carefully at the style of writing and any case studies that are included. This is the main benefit of going to a physical bookshop.

You can also browse similar books online, e.g. on Amazon. Amazon will show you what the bestselling titles are in your area and what readers think of them. Amazon is also a convenient means of checking whether someone else has used a title you have in mind. If so, you can gauge the existing book's popularity by its sales ranking. In some cases, it does not matter if you use the same title, particularly if you have a different subtitle, or if the other book is not selling well.

Some books are written only for the UK or the US market. You can increase your sales by adopting an international approach. One example is *The Tao of Coaching* by Max Landsberg, a former partner with McKinsey and Heidrick & Struggles.[1] It is a good idea to write for a global readership and test your manuscript on some non-native speakers of the language in which you are writing, if possible. The clearer your text, the easier it will be to translate.

You can still sell a lot of copies in one market, if your book meets a pressing need. A former colleague of ours, Semi Cho, wrote *Global Talent – How to Overcome Cultural Barriers and Become a Globally Competitive Professional*, in Korean.[2] The population of South Korea is 51 million – a little less than France or the UK. Nevertheless, her book appeals strongly to many Koreans' desire to work in international corporations or see their children do so. It sold 60,000 copies in its first 6 months and became a top-10 bestseller.

You may spot a gap in the market while you are looking for a book to recommend to other people. One author has done this with two books. Another was consistently told by his clients that he should write a book to help young people understand their passions so they could choose the right career.

Once you see an opportunity, you can estimate how big it is. How many people are potential purchasers and how badly do they need the book? Then you can choose a title that will appeal to them. You may change the title between now and publication, but having a working title gives you a sense of direction.

Publishers will want to know about the competition your book will face. It may actually help you if other writers have established a readership for your subject. If you have something new to say, people will buy your book, too. You can get an idea of how well other books are selling by looking on Amazon.

Publishers look for credible authors. They want manuscripts that are *authentic* – written by people who know their subject first hand and are experts in their field. There is much to be said for writing with a co-author. If you have similar values and expectations, you can produce a much better book than either of you would on your own. There will also be two of you to promote it once it is published. Our experience with *Brand You* is that $2 + 2 = 8$ (at least).

It is easy to write a turgid book on a subject you know well. It is harder, but a lot more fun, to write a book that brings your subject alive and makes it accessible to a wide readership. A good technique is to imagine you are going to read it aloud, with no visual aids. Listeners will want to understand it straight away, with no footnotes or further explanation. Otherwise, they will switch off. This approach also makes it easier to turn your manuscript into an audio book – tapping into another large and growing market.

If you base your book on material you have used to teach people, you will already know what they find most useful, most difficult, and so on. However, you will still need to experiment to ensure that readers enjoy the final version and recommend it to others. We do this by giving drafts to friends from different backgrounds and of various nationalities. The book evolves from one draft to the next.

If you are already well known, an autobiography or a book based on your experience and opinions can work extremely well. The bestseller lists in some countries contain lots of them. Politicians, generals, sportspeople and broadcasters have all written bestsellers in this genre – or have had them written for them. They have strong personal brands already, so publishers and readers flock to them. Even convicted criminals have succeeded.

Building a robust network

The way we network today has fundamentally changed. For the most part, in years gone by, networking was done largely face to face. However, increasingly, in recent years, networking is a mix of physical as well as digital. Here we will focus on the physical. In the following chapter on maintaining visibility online, we will look at how you network digitally.

Human beings have always had networks of relationships and contacts. However, these days many people's networks change and grow faster than before, due to frequent job moves, geographical mobility and the digital revolution. If you want to manage and build your brand, you have to manage and build your network both offline and online. But how?

Many of us still feel uncomfortable about cultivating a relationship, particularly face to face. It can feel as if you are a salesperson selling yourselvf in the hope of getting something from them. Guess what? You are not selling but rather marketing who you are, what you stand for and your talents and capabilities. Being your authentic self remains the best way to build your brand and increase your income.

Attracting a powerful network

Srikumar Rao, founder of The Rao Institute, has a useful technique for putting this into practice. It goes as follows:

- Stop trying to cultivate relationships with people you meet in the hope that they could be helpful to you.

- Next time you see, meet or hear about someone who is doing something that resonates with you, stop for a moment. It must be something that moves you. For example, they could be making television documentaries, turning around an ailing business or running a charity that helps violent offenders to lead a normal life. It is highly likely that you and that person have values in common.

- Send them a note or email explaining what excites you about what they do. Offer to help them in some specific way. Be prepared to go ahead if they accept your offer.

- Your intention is the key. You are not doing this because you want to form a relationship with them, it is because you believe in what they are doing.

- You will be surprised at how often your offer is accepted. As you fulfil your promise, a powerful network will begin to form around you, without your even having to try.

Opportunities for connecting

It is essential that if you choose to attend a face-to-face networking event, then you make sure that you are clear about what your reason for attending the event is. For example, how does it align with your overall purpose and, also, will the outcome(s) that you are seeking be met by attending this event?

Preparation and planning is key ahead of networking events. Identify the speakers and attendees ahead of the event so that you can decide who you would like to meet, why you would like to meet them and how you will approach them. Always have at the back of your mind how these individuals might add value to your brand. Can they help you to achieve your purpose? Where do your values align with theirs? What talents do you have that can best serve them?

If your intention is to secure a role in an organisation, then seek out as much information as possible about the culture of the organisation. How does it align with your brand? Does the culture fit with your purpose and what you hold as important? Overall, how does the culture align with your brand?

If you already have a role in an organisation and are seeking to extend your brand internally, then internal networks are a good way of doing this. Find out and explore networks that interest you and would provide you with a different set of connections as well as expand your knowledge in other areas.

At the end of the day, the raison d'être of networking events is opportunities to develop relationships, so consider differing and creative ways in which you could engage and develop current and new relationships. Here are a couple of examples:

- **Host your own events.** As well as keeping your brand at the forefront of minds, this gives you complete control over the attendees, the setting and the outcome. This type of event will add value by allowing you to present to current and potential clients, provide updates on your existing offer or on new research, tools or programmes.

- **Double date.** That is, invite others to join you the next time you have an open invitation or tickets to an event. This gives you the opportunity to deepen existing relationships and, if you have had the courage to reach out to those whom you don't know very well, and they accept your invitation, then you immediately have the opportunity to forge a new strategic partnership.

You can further utilise and deepen your network by reconnecting with people you have not seen for a while. As you've progressed with your career, your connections may become dormant for many reasons. Now may be the time to reconnect with former colleagues or classmates through channels such as LinkedIn or your customer relationship management (CRM) system. They are likely to have connections and knowledge that are different from your current network, and because you have a history with them, and perhaps even shared common interests, they will tend to be more open to your reach out.

Prudence is still essential – we are not suggesting you put detailed personal information online or invite complete strangers to events. However, it is important to be open with people if you want to find a new job, source a new assignment, or connect with others to develop talents, skills, ideas and businesses. As the saying goes, every opportunity begins with a relationship.

Business cards

Prior to the global pandemic, when we generally attended conferences and networking events in person, the standard engagement would include someone asking for your business card and saying, 'I'll email you my contact details.' Needless to say, very few did so.

In today's digital environment, digital business cards (also known as e-business cards or contactless business cards) have become more the norm. Digitalisation has changed how we keep in contact and connected with each other, and so the tools we use must reflect this and keep up with the times. (You could argue that digital cards are an online tool, but they are a replication of an offline tool, i.e. traditional printed cards. This is why we have chosen to cover them here, rather than in the following chapter).

There are three main benefits of digital business cards:

- First, you can share unlimited information. Because you are not forced to limit your details to comply with content space, it means that you are able to share multiple phone numbers, emails, website URLs, social media handles, Google Maps location, and much more. All of this information becomes accessible via a single screen tap.

- Second, digital cards can be updated as and when required. This means that, conveniently, there is no need to reprint the card if your contact information becomes outdated.

- Third, they are easily shared, as you can leverage quick and contactless card-sharing. Two further benefits include their financial viability, as you are reducing significant printing costs, and their eco-friendliness, as not using card helps towards a sustainable environment.

Business cards are 'nice to have' marketing paraphernalia. Almost background marketing material. And, if you would like to persevere with traditional business cards, ensure that they are clear and simple. That is, a business card that gives your full contact details, including your phone numbers, your email address and website URL. It should also remind people of who you are and what work you do. A useful tip is to keep the back of the card blank so you can write a message to remind people of the topic you discussed, or what each of you is going to do to follow up the initial conversation.

Key takeaways

- Building your brand offline is about visibly standing out.

- You stand out by being authentic. Authenticity is being able to show through your stories how your values, talents and skills combine to cement your presence.

- There are six key ways for you to increase the visibility of your brand offline:

  ○ Speaking engagements. Standing up, speaking and engaging with an audience provides credibility. Understand your audience's wants and needs and tune into what they would value listening to. Practise and try to relax and be authentic.

  ○ Television and radio offer maximum visibility. It is important to do your research to understand the audience's backgrounds. Whatever hooks you choose to focus in on, be mindful that they are context-related so that what you say cannot be misrepresented.

  ○ Being quoted in newspapers and magazines is a good way of creating a legacy and, if you are able to respond to journalists swiftly and are a reliable and accurate source, they will keep coming back to you for your input and material.

  ○ Writing letters to editors, contributing to articles, or publishing a book will raise your profile. Written material will always be available whether in hardcopy or online so ensure that your material is evidence-based and of high quality.

- ◦ It is easy for us to be in a comfort zone by staying at home and working virtually. However, the importance of connecting and building relationships and a significant network cannot be overstated. It allows people to gain a deeper understanding of who you are and what you stand for when they can look you in the eye and sense your spirit. Be clear that the events you attend align with your brand and how you will make the best use of these events to maximise your brand and aspirations.

- ◦ Many people, when they attend events, still like to have a reminder of who they meet and, more so, have a material memento of the interaction. This is where having business cards is helpful. Both digital and paper business cards should display all your contact details and, where possible, an indication of what you do so that you stand out!

Notes

1 Landsberg, M. (2015) *The Tao of Coaching: Boost Your Effectiveness at Work by Inspiring and Developing Those Around You*, Profile Books.

2 Cho, S. (2005) *Global Talent – How to Overcome Cultural Barriers and Become a Globally Competitive Professional*.

3 Rao, S. (2022) *Modern Wisdom Ancient Roots*, River Grove Books.

chapter 14

Building your brand online

In our ever-present digital and virtual world, your online presence extends from email, virtual meetings to websites blogs, vlogs, videos and reels, to podcasts, webinars, and to social media sites. All contribute to your digital networking efforts, and some would argue that your online presence can be more important than your offline presence as it provides you with global visibility that continuously evolves.

In this chapter, we'll take a look at each of these elements and begin from the position that standing out online is important for two reasons:

- First, your personality needs to come across virtually.

- Second, the wealth of information available online means that your brand has to be distinctive and consistent to stand out.

Again, it is important to be cognisant of the 'outside-in' presence of your brand and how it aligns with what you stand for and your unique set of skills and capabilities. Building your brand online allows you to truly explain what you do by crafting your stories through a variety of media so that your brand shines through, helping you to stand out against other candidates or competitors.

Email

Email now forms the bulk of our correspondence with one another. Therefore, it helps if your email address begins with your recognisable name. That way, if people have not contacted you for a while, they may find your email address right away when they type your full name into the address field on a blank email. Where possible, try to not use a nickname for your professional email address, even if close associates refer to you by your nickname. This will help you to maintain a consistent professional brand. Of course, your professional brand might include your nickname, in which case, a nickname is fine.

Some people's email addresses can be random, such as an initial followed by some unfathomable combination of numbers and letters, or the name of things such as their pet or house, which is only known to very close friends and colleagues. Any of these could lose you a potential client or employer as it may mean they spend time trawling through their inbox or 'deleted' folder, searching for an old message from you. More likely, they will give up looking.

If you have a common first name and/or surname, you can use your email address to remind people of who you are and what you do. For example: JoeBloggsWriter@gmail.com. Email is a good way to stay in touch and is less intrusive than phone calls. If your message has avoided the spam folder and is sitting in someone's inbox, they can read it whenever they want. However, be mindful of the volume of emails that many of us receive. As a result, there can be a tendency to delete unread emails, particularly if they appear as an obvious round robin marketing email. People are more likely to read yours if you personalise them with relevant information. For example, it helps if your email contains your full name and the subject line, a few descriptor words on the content; for example, *Urgent need to develop your talent acquisition process*.

Be clear on the objective of your emails. Would you like the recipient to gain interest in new work that you are offering that might interest them or would you like to remind them of your expertise and credibility in a particular area? Keep your emails short and simple. Get straight to the point of your content with a short intro, a few bulleted key points that avoid use of jargon, and offer to arrange a follow-up conversation.

If you are sending out a general marketing email to several contacts, then there are many useful online services for managing your email lists that will also enable you to mail merge emails to your contacts. You can then send Fred an email that begins 'Dear Fred' rather than 'Dear All' or 'Hi'. Fred is much more likely to pay attention. Finally, if it is a contact that you have met previously, in the first line of your email, remind them what links you together. For example, 'Dear Fred, I hope that you are keeping well? You must be delighted with the recent win of your football team' or 'I'm delighted to have read about your recent promotion', etc.

Virtual meetings

Today, more than ever, many of our meetings take place virtually. It is important that we pay attention to how we present ourselves in these meetings so that it aligns with our brand. How you look now can be quite different from your picture on your social media platform. Be mindful of this as it might lead others to question your authenticity. This not only signifies that your brand is inconsistent but also that you have not taken care to present yourself uniformly. This inadvertently can create a lack of trust in your brand.

Virtual meetings also provide an opportunity to add layers to who you are. Let's take our background screens as an example. Background screens are used for multiple reasons. For example:

- A blurred screen might be a way of hiding the fact that you are working from home.

- Your organisation might insist you used their preferred corporate background with their logo.

- Many choose their own background template which can be selected from standardised templates.

Over and above, be mindful of presenting yourself authentically. That is, if you are comfortable revealing your true background, then have courage to do so.

Other hygiene factors to be aware of when meeting virtually are:

- Test your system beforehand to ensure that the technology is working, i.e. WiFi, audio, etc.

- When setting up a meeting, ensure that the system provider does not boot you out if the meeting runs over.

- Ensure that the agenda is managed effectively so that all items can be covered in the allotted time.

- Be respectful of people's time by being punctual and aware of the time allocated for the meeting.

- If you are likely to be interrupted during the meeting, then advise others up front of this.

- Some people keep their screens turned off – this is not helpful as it makes it difficult to engage. Encourage them to be present by turning their video on. In this way, you become more attuned to non-verbal expressions and therefore able to respond appropriately. Also, when eye contact is maintained, it goes a long way towards building trust and developing a fruitful relationship with the other person.

- Be inclusive. Make sure that one person is not commandeering the meeting and that quiet individuals are drawn into the conversation.

Your Web presence

As the digital world continues to explode and grow, equally does the concept of Web presence. Web presence covers locations on the World Wide Web where a person, business or some other entity is represented. It includes the degree to which a website is visible in search engines and social media. Examples of a Web presence for a person could be a personal website, a blog, a profile page, a Wiki page or a social media profile. Web visibility can be measured by the number of visitors, keyword rankings and social media followers.

Many people's Web presence consists of a random series of mentions on various websites. The information can often be out of date and/or inaccurate. The first step, therefore, is to check your presence on the Web. If others share your name, then you need to think about how you differentiate yourself.

Exercise 23
Conduct an online brand audit

- -

1 Borrow someone else's computer, i.e. one that has no settings specific to you. Or clear all cookies on your own computer.

2 Type your full name, in inverted commas (e.g. 'Jo Smith'), into a search engine such as Google. See what comes up on the first page.

3 Add your name in inverted commas to Google Alerts. Go to www. google.com. Click on 'More', then 'Even more', then 'Alerts'. Then follow the instructions to receive alerts when new material about you (or someone with the same name as you) is published on the Web. If you share your name with others, then refine your alert to include key words or phrases that encompass what you do and how you stand out.

If the first page of results in (2) above leads to a website with your email address or phone number, that is an excellent start.

Now look at what has been written about you, and the context. Is this the brand image you wish to project? Will employers and clients be attracted by what they read?

- -

Visibility can be difficult if your name is a common one, such as Smith, Patel or Adeleke. One solution is to make sure you are mentioned in the context of what you do. If your name is John Smith and you are an architect, will people find you if they type 'John Smith' and 'architect' into Google? There may be nothing about you, but plenty about a namesake who is a notorious criminal.

If you do not like what you find written about you on the Web, you have three main options:

1 Sue people. We do not recommend this unless what they have written is clearly libellous. Getting into a fight will generate further negative publicity.

2 Become active online, generating positive, constructive comment about you that pushes the old, negative material further and further down the rankings. One of the best ways to do this is to start a blog in your own name and update it regularly. Unless you have a very common name, your blog will soon appear at or near the top of the Google ranking.

3 Hire an online reputation management service to do (2) above for you. There are many such organisations that are easy to find on the Web.

Building your brand online

Before immersing yourself fully in online marketing, it is best to be clear about what you wish to achieve. The archetypes discussed earlier in the book can help you do this.

Exercise 24
Your personal brand strategy

- -

Bring together the results of the exercises you have completed in this book.

Ask yourself the following questions:

1 What are my talents and values?

2 What is my unique combination?

3 Which archetypes do I evoke?

4 Who are the people I want to reach?

5 What do people want from me once they know I exist?

6 In view of my preferred archetype, which metaphors could I use to strengthen my brand online?

- -

Social networks allow you to evoke your archetype on a massive scale. For example, until now, you may have evoked the Jester only one to one or in small groups. With social media, you can reflect this to a much larger audience.

There is a lot of humour on social networking sites, just as there is in many homes and offices. If you are going to be humorous, it is best to do so in a way that comes naturally to you. It should be authentic and fit your personality. Some people naturally make off-the-cuff remarks and refer to this as 'banter', but be wary of how different cultural groups can perceive banter and how it can easily slip into, and tread the line of, insulting and, worse yet, discriminating.

You can also forward other people's material, including jokes and videos and make sure that you credit the original creator. It is important to consider which archetypes you are evoking when you do this. Dirty jokes will take you rapidly into Outlaw territory. Do you really want to do that in front of hundreds or thousands of people? Another option is to adopt a naïve approach to humour. That will take you closer to the Innocent.

Setting up a website

Personal websites have become more and more widespread, as a complement to your CV or business website. A personal website enables you to bring all your online activities together in one place. If possible, secure the 'vanity URL' (unique resource locator) for your online name or company name in it, as the authors have at www. davidroystonlee.com and www.globalintegrators.org.

You only have to give people one web address, i.e. yours, for them to find you on other social media sites. They will also find your blog, podcasts, books, audio recordings, video clips, etc. From there, you can direct them to other websites relating to your employer, any publications you may have written, other organisations you are involved with, and so on. With a website, you can bring all this together. It is best to include your first name and surname in the domain name, so your website is easy to find via Google and other search engines.

If you are self-employed, then it is important that potential clients and known colleagues and associates can find and contact you. Potential clients may expect you to have a website and assume you are no good if you do not. If you have both a personal and a business website, make sure their messages are consistent, with a similar look and feel.

If you are a media star, a website will help your fans to follow your progress without getting too close. You can also use it to sell your knowledge material or merchandise.

Not everyone wants a website. Some angel investors prefer to keep a low profile. It helps them to avoid being mobbed by entrepreneurs seeking finance. Some salaried employees shudder at the thought of setting up a website. They fear it will smack of self-promotion and send the wrong message to their boss. However, it does not have to be that way. For example, an increasing number of people write blogs about their area of expertise in a way that helps to attract and retain customers for their employers. These blogs can be either on the company's website or on a personal website.

Another example might be people who are returning to work following a significant period of time off. A website may be a way of complementing the brand that you had and building upon it.

A personal website can be particularly useful if you are between jobs, i.e. unemployed. It will help you to continue commenting on your chosen field and interacting with people who are involved in it. It will make you more visible to potential employers, business partners, and so on.

Whether your website is focused on you or on a particular topic, it helps to have an 'About' page, with a description of who you are and what you do – and a photograph in which you come across as friendly and approachable. A short video of you can be even more powerful. You can post it on YouTube and then embed it in your website or blog posts.

You can use your website to communicate your unique combination of talents, skills and experience through the text and the illustrations. Your brand identity is more subtle, but no less important.

We introduced the metaphors that support your brand in Chapter 9 on archetypes. Imagine you are a medical specialist who cures back injuries. Metaphors that evoke the Magician and the Caregiver may be more aligned with your brand. We are not advocating a photograph of you wearing a pointed hat and waving a wand. What we are advocating is that your website will be more powerful if the vocabulary you use in it evokes the Magician or Caregiver. For instance, you could use words such as *transform* or *protective* to help strengthen your brand identity. Similarly, you could include a page of tips to help people stay healthy. This will help to reinforce your brand.

If you are a fitness coach or personal trainer, metaphors that evoke the Hero archetype might fit your brand and be used in your website. You could have pictures of muscular men and women straining every sinew in pursuit of glory. However, that may not reflect what you do for your clients. Many people hire a personal trainer to make them stick to an exercise regime, so they lose weight and get fit. In other words, they may want to see wording that evokes the Ruler. You could evoke the Ruler by having pictures of fit, athletic people in suits, striding up the steps to the entrance of a large corporation, with an architrave supported by Doric columns. Or, you could include guidelines for healthy eating and exercise planners that people can download from your website.

If appropriate, you can mention your existing clients. The stronger their brands, the more yours will benefit. Links to other websites are crucial. They give people a reason to keep visiting your site and use it as a point of reference. When linking your website to others, make sure the connection enhances your brand. The quality of the sites, and the values they express, should be consistent with your own. The more useful you make your website, the more likely people are to add it to their favourites list.

Unless you are an accomplished web designer, you will likely need professional help with your site. Pay a web developer to tailor the software to your requirements. Since they will not have to build a website from scratch, this is much cheaper than the traditional approach, which used to cost thousands of pounds. These days, a presentable website with a blog and links to social media sites should cost only a few hundred pounds.

Another clever way to do this is to seek students who study this and work with them to build your website. Their fee is often much less than a website design company.

Alternatively, if you are technically inclined, you can set up and build a website with a blog free of charge at www.wordpress.com or www.wizz.com. This is an easy way to get started. You will need to pay for a domain name and hosting. In creating your website, there is no need to go overboard. Time-consuming animation, for example, can be counterproductive, since many people find it annoying. If they cannot *skip intro*, they may give up and go elsewhere.

The text is really important. Since this is a personal site, you may be able to adopt an informal style that reflects the way you speak, which will help your personality to come across. Ask someone to check the grammar and spelling. Then show a pilot version to a few people before it goes live. What is their first impression? How do they feel about what they see? Make sure your site is easy to navigate, so people keep coming back. It's worth including third-party endorsements and articles that mention you.

Once your site is up and running, it helps if people can find it quickly when they Google you. Your site's ranking will be determined by a number of factors that change from time to time.

These include the number of links with other sites. You or your web designer can find out more about this in *Search Engine Optimization for Dummies* by Peter Kent.[1]

If you are employed and appear on a corporate website, make sure it conveys the right message. If possible, check any material that mentions you before it goes live. Try printing out any pages that include your biography or photograph. The result may be very different from what you see on the screen. Photos can come out in many different sizes. Is your photo up-to-date and accurate? If you have aged 15 years or dyed your hair a different colour, it could cause confusion or embarrassment when you meet people face to face.

Content marketing to build your brand

Content marketing involves the creation and sharing of online material such as videos, blogs, podcasts, webinars and social media posts. If you ensure that your purpose, values and talents are clear, then it can explicitly promote your brand and stimulate interest in your products or services.

Blogs and vlogs

Blog is short for *weblog*: effectively an online diary located on a website. Vlog is a form of blog for which the medium is video. Blogs and vlogs first appeared in the late 1990s and 2000, respectively. Bloggers write text, sometimes accompanied by pictures and audio recordings, and vloggers tell their stories through videos that can deliver context through imagery and sound as opposed to written blogs.

People who read your blog and watch your vlogs can choose to subscribe to it. They will then receive new material via email or RSS (popularly known as really simple syndication), which sends it to their device. They may also be able to leave comments on your blog/vlog, which you can either approve or reject.

You can set up a blog/vlog for free on sites such as WordPress (www.wordpress.com), Blogger (www.blogger.com) and YouTube (www.youtube.com). However, if you want to build a strong personal brand online, it is often better to host your blog/vlog on your own website with your own domain, i.e. a website name that does not include the name of the blogging software. This shows that you are making a serious commitment to your blog/vlog and your online presence in general. It also gives you more flexibility. You can design the blog/vlog the way you want it or pay someone else to do so. Having your own domain also makes it easier for you or someone you nominate to improve your ranking on Google and elsewhere using search engine optimisation (SEO). The *For Dummies* series, published by John Wiley & Sons, has several books on blogging that will help you get started.

You can use websites such as Facebook, Substack, LinkedIn, Pinterest, Reddit, StumbleUpon, TikTok, Instagram, and Twitter to promote your blog/vlog. Be wary that the popularity of these sites changes constantly. For instance, in May 2022, Instagram and TikTok surpassed Facebook in terms of people signing up.

Many people have made good use of blogs/vlogs to establish and maintain a connection with their fans, clients, customers or investors. Some also sell products directly from their websites. A good example of this is goop.com by the actress Gwyneth Paltrow, which began as a blog.

Celebrities often use their full names for their websites, blogs and vlogs. This makes sense if they have already built a big brand offline. Their fans can then find them easily online. If you happen not to be a celebrity, you may find that you can build a bigger and more valuable following by focusing on a subject that you are enthusiastic about. It is best if there is a clear benefit to visiting your blog/vlog, such as entertainment, useful information or solutions to a particular kind of problem.

One proven way to build a following for your blog/vlog is to create great content and build relationships with other people who blog/vlog on closely related subjects. You can start by commenting (intelligently) on their blogs. Later on, you may link your websites to each other. You can interview or be interviewed by them. You can write guest posts on each other's blogs/vlogs. It is rather like television channels whose ratings are determined partly by the people who agree to appear on particular chat shows. Being provocative online can often pay off as people love to listen to someone with a contrary opinion and it can make you stand out.

Once your blog/vlog is popular, you can use search engine optimisation (SEO) to help people find it or hashtags (#). This will help improve its ranking when people search on related topics using Google, for example. Even the headlines you use on your blog will affect its ranking. If you include keywords that people are likely to enter as search terms, they are more likely to find your blog/vlog. You can either invest the necessary time and energy to learn SEO, or you can hire someone who is already an expert on the subject.

Starting a blog or vlog is a commitment since it should, ideally, be updated at least once a week to be effective. (Google likes fresh content.) Some people update theirs three to five times per week. It gives their readers a reason to keep coming back for new posts. The simplest way to think of a blog is as your journal where you choose to make a regular entry.

If you update your blog/vlog only occasionally, it may become more like an online newsletter. In this case, it is worth ensuring that all the content is accurate, both factually and grammatically, just like any other brochure. It is also helpful to include 'share' buttons that enable people to tell their friends about your blog on the main social networking sites described below.

The more strongly your blog/vlog uses metaphors that identify the authentic you (which you identified in Chapter 9 on archetypes), the easier it will be to build a following. A blog can be a great place to publish and test new ideas, which you can then turn into a book. Those who subscribe to the blog are likely to buy your book and/or recommend it to others.

Newsletters

A newsletter is an email sent periodically that informs your audience of the latest news, tips or updates relating to your products or services. Newsletters help to share material that corresponds specifically with your areas of expertise and interests.

It is widely accepted that there are five key components of a quality newsletter:

- readability, in that time-constrained audiences can scan newsletters for exciting ideas and relevant information
- storytelling value
- reader focus
- have a clear call to action
- attractive, user-friendly design.

Readers are particularly likely to subscribe if you offer them some free material in return.

Videos and reels

Videos and reels can be a useful personal branding tool for people in a wide range of occupations, and YouTube, Instagram and TikTok are social media sites that enable these tools.

Reels allow you to share creative, entertaining content. They tend to be more interactive and engaging. With video you are more likely to share educational and in-depth content. No matter which format you choose, make sure your content is informative.

If you are paid as a speaker, actor or musician, potential clients will be able to see you perform. If you are a film-maker, you can upload short examples of your work. A wide range of people find it helpful to embed YouTube videos into their websites, so viewers can get a sense of who they are while they are delivering their message.

People have launched successful careers on YouTube, Instagram and TikTok, sometimes from their bedrooms. For instance, Justin Bieber, Billie Eilish and KSI all began by uploading their music onto social media.

If you use a search engine, such as Google, videos and reels often appear on the front page (it is worth bearing in mind that YouTube is owned by Google).

Rather than always writing text for your blog, you may prefer to make a video and insert it into your blog. This has several advantages:

- Videos and reels help people to grasp who you are as a person. They will relate to you more easily and feel more comfortable doing business with you. Some people find videos and reels far more engaging than photographs or text.

- If you are an expert on a particular subject and upload videos and reels of yourself speaking to live audiences, you are likely to receive invitations to speak elsewhere. Becoming a professional speaker can boost your income as well as strengthen your brand in terms of both reach and reputation.

- It gives you another way to engage with your audience. Some people prefer to watch a video or reel rather than read about what you do.

- YouTube is also a great tool for researching any subject that interests you. Experts often upload their latest presentations at conferences around the globe to cater to these browsers.

Podcasts and webinars

Podcasts are audio files that people can download and listen to. They are mainly used to establish yourself as an expert in your field, or to share a lifestyle or experience that can offer guidance and information. For example, if your podcast relates to a shared experience such as grief or going through a life-changing event, then your brand evokes the Caregiver. It is a particularly flexible tool as an audience can listen to it anywhere at any time.

Webinars are typically educational. They are multimedia meetings held over the internet and done in real time. They are a good way to gain insight of up-to-date information and you can talk to your audience and receive feedback from them instantly. Webinars are also useful in that you can share presentations and screens, conduct surveys, use chat features and earn money on the spot if you are selling a product or service.

Often, podcasts and webinars are used together. Podcasts attract interest and webinars provide deeper insight into your service or product offering and extend the relationship with people who may want to use your services.

Using social media to build your brand

Prior to the advent of technology, digitisation and social media, social interactions took place mainly offline: at home, at work, on the phone and in cafés, bars and restaurants. With the advent of social media, more and more of these interactions are taking place online, in front of hundreds, thousands or even millions of people. Just as with TV and radio, you can tune in and out whenever you want. In other words, the internet, and social media in particular, has helped to make networking easier than ever before.

LinkedIn, Instagram, YouTube, Twitter, TikTok and Facebook are examples of social media sites. However, please be wary that the popularity of these sites ebb and flow. For example, MySpace, popular some time ago, is now redundant. Similarly, social sites may be dependent on generation. So, many TikTokers may not ever visit Facebook and vice versa. The important point here is that it is not solely about followers, it is about getting known and accepted within your target market.

Making full use of social media

The implications of social media for personal branding are enormous and, understandably, there is confusion about how to use social media. Some sceptics say they have no interest in reading about what someone had for breakfast, therefore the whole thing is a waste of time. However, the same could be said of radio, television and many newspapers and magazines. There is a torrent of information throughout the media, both on- and offline. The key is to clarify your message and find a way to connect with your audience.

As with anything new, we learn partly through trial and error. One common problem arises if you behave in one way online and in another way offline. You can end up evoking a wide range of archetypes and leaving people confused about who you really are.

Some people do things on social networking sites that they would never do elsewhere. For example, the wife of the head of MI6, Britain's secret service, posted a photo of him in his swimming trunks on Facebook, together with the address of their apartment and the whereabouts of their three children. The photo was then picked up by the press and widely circulated.

Social networking sites are like any other tool. They can be used well or badly. This book will help you do the former.

If you have completed the exercises in this book, you will have an understanding of yourself and the message you want to put across. In order to communicate effectively online, it helps to understand the media in question. In this section, we will focus on digital platforms that can promote your brand such as social media sites (e.g. LinkedIn, Instagram, Twitter, TikTok and Facebook). This section is a brief description of each.

Social media sites

Social media is a way of life now and many social media sites have their unique focus. For example, LinkedIn (www.linkedin.com) describes itself as a professional network rather than a social one.

On average, two new people join every second for the purpose of extending their network.

Instagram, TikTok, Twitter and Facebook continue to be popular social media sites with their own identity, purpose and reach. There also continues to be a stealth of digital media and tools that continue to come onto the market such as Slack and Substack. The key is to know which one suits your purpose.

LinkedIn

The first element of LinkedIn that you need to attend to is your profile. If all you do is transcribe your CV onto LinkedIn and upload a photo of yourself in business attire, you risk being two-dimensional. Instead of your brand being a tall, distinctive building that is visible for miles around, it will be one of those grey ones that almost no one notices as they go past.

It is best to summarise what you do in a short and memorable way. For example, instead of describing yourself as 'Marketing manager at Whizzo Media', you might write 'Digital marketing specialist for high-growth media companies'. People need to know what you do, which is not the same thing as your job title. Your headline is probably the most important section of your profile. For example, the authors' headlines are:

David Royston-Lee:

Senior Leadership Coach and Branding Expert, Chairman of Future Resume. Author

Sylvana Storey:

Corporate Culture, Leadership & Diversity & Inclusion Provocateur | Business Psychologist | OD Specialist | Author | Keynote Speaker

Pay particular attention to the keywords that you use in your profile heading. This enables hiring firms, as well as potential employers and clients, to find you by searching the entire LinkedIn database swiftly. Also, another feature on LinkedIn you may wish to leverage is 'Talks about', which allows others to know exactly what subject areas you are an expert in or specialise in.

LinkedIn adds new features all the time, partly in response to competition from other websites. The 'Skills' section in your profile is particularly useful, since it is close to the unique combination of talents, skills and experience that you have worked on. You can choose them from a drop-down menu. For example:

David Royston-Lee:

Career strategy, personal branding, psychology, published author, executive coaching, leadership mentoring

Sylvana Storey:

Culture change, psychology; executive coaching, organisational development; leadership development and diversity and inclusion

Now you have read through this book and completed the exercises, you are likely to be able to write a much better explanation of who you are on LinkedIn. You can explain what you do, how you do it and what you want to do.

After networking, recruitment remains a key aspect of LinkedIn. Headhunters and hiring companies are increasingly using LinkedIn to complement their own databases. If they do not already have a candidate's CV or contact details, they can usually find them on LinkedIn. Make sure the dates, job titles, etc. on your LinkedIn profile match those on the CV that you give to potential employers. Elsewhere on LinkedIn, it is good to talk about what you *want* to do and not just what you *have* done.

Other elements and activities particular to LinkedIn and those that you can consider include: joining groups, inviting people to events, endorsing colleagues, getting recommendations from former clients and bosses. You can also add your own material, such as creating articles and newsletters,

SlideShare presentations, documents, videos and your latest blog posts as well as re-share others' material. All of these can help to create the right impression when people visit your LinkedIn page.

Instagram

Instagram (www.instagram.com) is a social networking service that connects your message with a photo, video story and/or reel that stirs and evokes a visual memory of what you do. It enables you to build a community, build influence and create compelling content that's distinctly yours. The app allows users to upload media that can be edited with filters and organised by hashtags and geographical tagging. Posts can be shared publicly or with preapproved followers.

TikTok

TikTok (www.tiktok.com) is the fastest growing social media site at the time of writing. Worldwide, currently, the TikTok app has been installed 3 billion times and boasts 1 billion active users on a monthly basis. In the Chinese market, TikTok works as a separate app called Douyin, which is one of the most popular apps in the country.

TikTok is a video-sharing app that allows users to create and share short-form videos on any topic and provides great visibility. It is mainly mobile-based, although you can still watch TikTok videos using the web app. The platform allows users to get creative with their content using filters, stickers, voiceovers, sound effects and background music. Videos can be recorded, uploaded and edited and reels can be informative and educational as well as provide funny sketches, dance and entertainment. You can creatively express your brand story, educate your audience and get discovered by people who may love your business. Many viral trends and challenges are often kickstarted on TikTok and, importantly, the app has a live stream capability so you can reach your audience in present time.

Twitter

Twitter's (www.twitter.com) unique focus is brevity. A *tweet*, in which you can use a maximum of 280 characters, ensures that your message is short and to the point. Twitter operates in real time and allows for differing viewpoints. You can also search to see which topics are 'trending', i.e. being discussed by millions of people worldwide. The *hashtag* (#) enables you to highlight key content and to find people who share your interests and communicate with them online.

Facebook

Facebook (www.facebook.com) remains one of the largest social networking sites but is slowly being associated with boomers and Gen X and is less appealing to Millennials and Gen Z. Most people prefer to use it for their personal lives and, in this vein, increasingly, employers and potential business partners will look at your Facebook page, so be careful what you upload! It is also important to note that Facebook also gives you the opportunity to set up a business page.

Getting started with social media

To get started with social media, we suggest you do the following:

1 If you have a URL (unique resource locator), link this to all your social media sites, if possible. This is the URL that includes your business name or company name, for example: https://www. facebook.com followed by your name/organisation; https://www. instagram.com followed by your name/organisation.

2 Where possible, it will be helpful to have the same name across all the main social media platforms. Consistency will help people to find you and connect with you easily.

On LinkedIn and Twitter this will happen automatically when you open your account. On other platforms your name may be already taken. If this is the case, try to create a name that is close to your name, or combine your name with the name of your business.

3 Complete your social media profiles. All you need right now is the basic information. Once your profile is up and running, it will improve your Google ranking when people search for you online. In the bio you can include hyperlinks to your pages on other sites, such as Facebook, LinkedIn, Twitter and YouTube, as well as to your blog. You can choose which part of your profile is visible from a random search on Google and which part is visible only to your friends and family, for example.

4 Get a professional head-and-shoulders photo that you can use on all websites. While you are about it, it is worth asking for some with plain white backgrounds, as this will not clash with other colours you may be wearing. Editors of other websites will find them useful if they write an article about you.

Think about who you are trying to reach

Depending on your security settings, anyone anywhere in the world could be reading what you write online. You may wish to ignore this fact and write purely for your local market, or for a group of people who share your outlook and/or interests. However, if you are targeting a global market, it is worth considering cultural differences.

In some cultures, it is considered normal and acceptable to promote yourself and tell everyone how great you are. In others, this is considered boastful and rude, so people with much to offer are silent and practically invisible on the Web. If you find yourself at either extreme, you may wish to adapt your style and move closer to the middle. Then you can appeal to a global audience. Also, be wary of the language and, in particular, jargon that you use. What might appear normal in your culture might be offensive in another.

If you build a large following online, it is rather like having your own TV or radio station. When you go to meetings or social events, people will comment on what you have written online and the discussions that have arisen out of it. You may discover that people read more of your material online than you had realised – they may simply choose not to comment on it.

Using technology to manage your network

Many of us have hundreds or even thousands of contacts on social networking sites. Some we know personally and some we do not. You can use contact-management software on your computer and/ or your smartphone to keep track of those you know personally. This has the advantage that you can send a message to all of them at once when you need to, for example, when you change jobs. Your IT department or an IT consultant can show you how to synchronise the information in your smartphone with that held in your computer. Your mobile network provider may also be able to help.

Fine-tuning your approach

Using a new medium always involves a certain amount of trial and error. One of the advantages of social media is that you get rapid feedback. If you say something on Twitter that people like, some will tell you so. If they do not like it, they will unfollow or even block you and often tell you so.

Here are some further tips:

- You can save yourself a lot of time and anxiety if you work on the assumption that anything you post online is public. Even if you post something among friends and family with maximum security settings, someone can still cut and paste what you have written and post it anywhere they want on the Web. Importantly, this includes private information such as your date and place of birth, travel plans or home address.

- Talk about your business, product or service only now and then. It is best to spend a significant amount of your time providing material that your audience will enjoy, without trying to sell them anything. It is rather like commercial television – an advertisement now and then is acceptable; if there are too many of them, people get bored and switch off. The aim of building your brand online is to engage with people and make sure they remember you when they have a need that you may be able to meet. In the meantime, you want them to keep coming back to you online for free updates.

- It is much easier to stand out if you write and speak authentically. In other words, you should be yourself in all media and in real life. People will warm to you if they can see what they perceive as your faults as well as your good points. The psychologist Carl Jung said: 'I'd rather be whole than good.' If you think about the most successful people in the conventional media, such as musicians, sportspeople, broadcasters and film stars, their fans are all too aware of their failings. However, they love them all the same. Most of us relate to people who are human rather than perfect and therefore artificial.

- Make sure what you say is true and accurate. Would you be comfortable saying it to a complete stranger the first time you met them?

- Comment on blogs in your field. You can usually tell which are the most popular by looking at the number of retweets, shares and blog comments. Popular blogs automatically get a high Google ranking. Having said all of this, when you are commenting on other people's blogs, the priority is to build a relationship with the bloggers and their contacts.

- When people comment on your posts or your blog, be sure to reply to their comments, where appropriate. Some people treat social media like old-fashioned broadcasting: they send their message out into the world and then ignore what anyone says in response. This can make them look out of touch or arrogant. It is much better to engage with your audience and acknowledge them. If you are helpful and sincere, you can build a relationship with some of them. Your following will begin to grow. This is especially true on your blog. When you reply to people's comments, a virtuous circle develops, making your blog look and become more and more popular.

- Comment on other people's posts with care. Some people might like it when you read what they write and respond constructively. Others, dependent on your brand, might appreciate humour. For example, if your brand evokes the Jester – using humour to get a serious point across.

Measuring the results

Measuring the results of your social media strategy can be useful depending on your trade. For example, if you are an influencer or service provider, it might be helpful to know your audience and your reach to enable follow through and tailored messaging. You can monitor your visitors using Google Analytics, for example. This service shows you the number of visits your website has received each day, which pages were viewed and whether people visited your site directly or via a search engine or referral site. Google Analytics also enables you to see each visitor's country of origin.

Protecting and extending your brand

Although your brand is an *intangible* asset, it could easily become more valuable than any *physical* asset you possess. It is therefore worth protecting.

Managing your brand name(s)

The steps you take to protect your personal brand name will depend partly on how famous you are, or intend to become. If you decide to be visible on the Web, it is best to register your domain name across as many suffixes as possible. For example: .com, .co.uk, .org. You may even choose to register your name and logo as a trademark.

Treat people fairly

New ventures are always risky, whether they are in the theatre, the cinema, technology, consumer products, retailing or elsewhere. However, you can ensure that everyone involved knows the risks they are taking and is treated fairly. You can also make sure, before you take on a project, that you have the time and resources required to do an excellent job. If you have to cancel the whole thing, or close down a business, you can do so ethically and transparently.

Some people damage their brands without thinking about it. They gain in the short term but lose in the long term. If you behave impeccably, you will keep attracting people and new opportunities. You will be much better off overall.

Take the initiative – deal with problems straightaway

If people in your network share your values, you should have few problems. However, if they do anything that could damage your brand, you may have to distance yourself. Turning a blind eye is a big risk. It may be enough to tell them how uncomfortable you feel about what is going on. The advantage of saying how you feel is that no one can contradict you. Neither have you judged them nor accused them of anything.

If they are doing something illegal, it is worth consulting a lawyer. You may wish to resign or terminate your relationship. The longer you allow things to continue, the greater the potential damage to your brand. The business world and politics offer many examples of reputations and entire careers blighted by scandal. If it emerges that you acted swiftly when you found out what was going on, it may even *enhance* your brand.

Extending your brand

Brands are not single products or services. A brand is a symbol that guarantees a particular experience. Brands give meaning to life and can take many forms. They can be extended to new products and services, provided the *essence* of the brand is maintained.[2] As Andy Milligan points out in his book, *Brand It Like Beckham*: 'Once people experience a brand and like it, it acquires the legitimacy to offer them something else: maybe a different kind of product, but one with similarities in form or function or emotional resonance.'

Successful corporate brands have done this for many years. Virgin started as a record company. The brand has since been extended to air travel, financial services, mobile phones and many other products and services. The Easy brand has been extended from easyJet to easyCruise and beyond. Brands can be extended if they make and fulfil a strong promise to customers, with a consistent purpose and set of values.

The same applies to your brand. If you are thinking of doing something new, ask yourself whether it will fit your purpose and your values. Will it evoke the same archetype as before? Imagine your brand is a tall building with a large atrium. When visitors enter at street level, they immediately get a feel for its purpose. It might be a department store selling everything for the home. There are counters and shop assistants everywhere. When visitors look up, they see balconies on the floors above. Your department store can add any product range that is consistent with your purpose and your values.

It is best to extend your brand to areas where you are credible or can become so quickly. One author has a background as a psychologist and was previously a human resources director, a chief executive and a management consultant. They now draw on all this experience to help organisations and their senior people to clarify their mission and market themselves more effectively.

The other author extends their background in business psychology to advise on wider organisational issues, deliver keynotes and write books.

Exercise 25
Extending your brand

- -

Write down, in as much detail as you can, everything you enjoy doing and do well. Include the things you do at work and in your spare time. What are the underlying talents? What are the values that make those activities meaningful for you? Write down all the other talents you have discovered in yourself and enjoy using, but are not using right now.

Now make a list of new activities you would like to try. Could you begin any of them now? Would they enhance your brand?

- -

Experimenting with and extending your brand helps you maintain a high level of energy. It keeps you at the forefront of what interests you most.

The Beckham family: case study 1 in brand extension

The Beckhams are a good example of how to build a global brand and extend it beyond the original activity. Some of the material in this case study is taken from Andy Milligan's book, *Brand It Like Beckham – The Story of How Brand Beckham Was Built*. If you are interested in personal branding and/or football, we highly recommend it.

Let us begin with David Beckham, who has been successful in building a global brand by evoking two archetypes: the Magician and the Ordinary Person. With the Magician we know that he may not be the greatest footballer the world has ever seen, but he is exceptionally skilful, often transforming his team's fortunes. With the Ordinary Person, he strengthens his

---

appeal to people who feel that he is 'just like me'. His lack of fluency in his mother tongue is consistent with the Ordinary Person and has made people warm to him. When asked by a journalist if he was learning Japanese in time for the 2002 World Cup, he replied: 'I'm still tryin' English.'

The key to his brand is consistency. Evoking these two archetypes consistently has enabled David Beckham to build a unique brand that is admired around the world by men and women, young and old and extend his brand across several product categories and achieve an unusual level of commercial success.

Victoria Beckham's brand has also consistently evolved. As Victoria Adams in the Spice Girls, 'Posh Spice', to marrying David, to recreating her career to a successful fashion designer and becoming a fashion icon, together they have spread the Beckham brand to a wider audience.

Further, their four children are on their way to capitalising on, and extending, their parents' brand.

Marcus Rashford: case study 2 in brand extension

Marcus Rashford, a star football player for Manchester United and the England squad, is a campaigner against racism, homelessness and child hunger in the United Kingdom. His experiences as a child growing up in Manchester with a single parent have influenced his philanthropy efforts and political activism to drive societal change. Particularly, he has used his platform to campaign the UK Government to end child poverty, specifically, for government to provide free meals to children in financially struggling families during the school holidays nationwide. His campaign is credited with

➤

government funding, almost £400 million in a 12-month period, to support the cost of food and household bills to poor families. For his efforts, he has received widespread praise and has been recognised for his efforts from organisations both in and outside of sport.

Be selective about endorsements and recommendations

If you are well-known, you may have opportunities to endorse products and services. If you choose them carefully, they can strengthen your brand as well as generate extra revenue. However, they must fit your brand image. For example, former endorsements of *Brand You* included:

- 'I was lucky enough to read this book just as I was rethinking my career. It proved invaluable.' Social Media Consultant.

- 'We find *Brand You* an invaluable tool for helping top performers become leaders in their sectors.' CEO.

Key takeaways

- Email forms the bulk of our correspondence. Endeavour to use your recognisable name and be clear on the objective of your email. Keep your communication simple and to the point.

- In an increasingly hybrid and global working environment, it has become more usual to meet virtually. In this setup, ensure that your image is consistent across all platforms and be mindful of protocols and etiquette when attending virtual meetings.

- So as to increase your visibility through web presence, consider setting up a personal website. A personal website enables you to bring all your online activities together in one place and maximises the visibility of your brand. It also allows you to provide information that you choose to offer that people may find of value.

- Content marketing is a great way to increase your presence online, and the material that you provide can set you apart from your colleagues or competitors alike. You can establish a distinctive brand using your own voice through blogs, vlogs, videos and reels, newsletters, podcasts and webinars.

- Social media sites are popular and include LinkedIn, Instagram, TikTok, Twitter and Facebook. They each have their own identity, purpose and reach but their key advantage is their ability to reach global audiences.

- There continues to be a stream of digital media and tools that continue to come onto the market such as Slack and Substack. The key is to know which one suits your purpose.

Notes

1 Kent, P. (2008) *Search Engine Optimization for Dummies*, John Wiley &Sons.

2 Milligan, A. (2010) *Brand it like Beckham*, Marshall Cavendish.

chapter 15

Aligning your CV and covering letter with your brand

This chapter covers how you position yourself in the world through your CV and covering letters.

The exercises that you have worked on as you progressed through this book have developed your awareness of who you are and how you can evoke your brand in line with your aspirations. Without doing the exercises and learning more about how you want to work a CV it is just a one-dimensional piece of paper.

Before updating your CV, we need to bring everything you have learned about yourself together to ensure what you write in your CV reflects the authentic you.

We have used the image of a building in previous chapters to develop your understanding of your purpose, values and talents. A CV is like a snapshot of that building that shows enough of you to entice the viewer to want to know more about you and therefore contact you.

This chapter will provide a way of preparing what you need to put a CV together as well as offer examples of how you could structure different types of CVs and covering letters.

Before we delve into the traditional CV, we think that it is important to reflect on where you are and what you have achieved so far in your life.

Reflecting on your journey so far

One way of bringing all the information about yourself together is to write what the authors term a Future Resume. As a precursor to writing your CV, this document collates your aspirations and ambitions, showcasing your talents, values and what you enjoy doing, and emphasises the kind of work that would satisfy you.

It helps you to take a future perspective on all you have learned from the past, enabling you to focus on who you are, the type of work you would like to do and where you want to be.

In the exercise below, we encourage you to bring what you have learnt from the past together with your future ambitions and aspirations. This is what we term a Future Resume format.

Exercise 26
Future Resume format

- -

Having identified where you were, we are now looking at your development into the future.

What are the key values that you need for the future?

. . . .

. . . .

. . . .

What are the talents that you would like to develop further into the future?

. . . .

. . . .

. . . .

What skills are you most proud of and still want to develop?

. . . .

. . . .

. . . .

Looking back over your life, what do you enjoy doing and what are you good at?

. . . .

. . . .

. . . .

What experiences have helped you to be the person you are?

. . . .

. . . .

. . . .

What environments suit you best?

. . . .

. . . .

. . . .

What qualifications might you need for the future?

. . . .

. . . .

Looking at your life so far, what are the biggest challenges you have faced?

. . . .

. . . .

. . . .

What kind of work would satisfy you in the future?

. . . .

. . . .

. . . .

What areas of life do you want to work on so that you can be the best version of yourself?

. . . .

. . . .

What do you want to achieve in your life?

. . . .

. . . .

. . . .

Looking at your life so far, what stories can you share that show both the present and future you?

. . . .

. . . .

. . . .

By reflecting on your answers, you will have clarified in your mind the following: how the past has shaped you, where you are presently, and where you would like to go.

These insights help you to prepare your CV based on your past, present and future. This account enables your CV to be authentic.

Adapted from Future Resume Ltd. Used by permission.

Stories to support your CV

By reflecting on the exercise above, you are in a good place to write an authentic CV. You now need to think about the stories that support what you say about yourself in the CV.

For instance, in an interview, you are often asked to discuss the challenges that you have faced and how you have learnt from them. You may also be asked what you are most proud of and why.

Your story is the narrative that supports your CV. Below are two examples of stories that show situations and/or challenges that needed to be addressed and the outcome in terms of learnings.

Story 1

Having worked in a number of business areas across my current organisation, I realised four years ago that I had to move to a project team for future career development within the organisation. First, I requested a shadowing opportunity in a project team. Once I did that, I decided to gain a formal project qualification and enrolled for a PRINCE2 Practitioner course that I completed in June 2013. I was desperately looking for project opportunities and finally became successful in securing a project management role in September 2013.

I was really motivated to change my role, moving my career in a different direction. I was successful in doing that. I learned that it's possible to achieve what I want if the real determination and commitment are there.

Story 2

I recently stood for an election in my organisation in order to be the vice-chair of a staff network group.

➤

I put forward my nomination, getting approval from my line manager. I did a targeted campaign once I was chosen as a candidate. I tried to make colleagues members, with a view to making them eligible to vote. I sent some generic emails to people I knew over the years.

Unfortunately, my bid was unsuccessful. The lessons for me were threefold. First, my personal statement targeting eligible voters was too detailed and not focused enough. Second, I only looked at the bid from my perspective and not the voters, which impacted on how I engaged with them. Third, personalised emails rather than a generic email would have been a better approach to gain more trust and form a relationship that would get more votes.

This helped me to realise how I engaged with people, which proved to be a huge benefit for future opportunities.

The traditional CV

Using the Future Resume exercise above, you can now utilise your responses to create or update a more traditional CV. Your CV funnels what you have learnt into specific areas of interest. It drills down into key career expectations and aligns these with your experiences and achievements.

Most people have a CV that uses a standard template to chronicle their career and acquired skills over time. However, their CVs are often not structured or aligned to their personal brand. By doing the work to understand your purpose, values, talents and skills, as well as clarifying your aspirations, your brand will be clear to you and to others.

Whether you are creating an entirely new CV or refreshing your CV, it is important to be mindful of the recipient. A tailored CV will help to better engage with the hiring manager by aligning your experience and capabilities with what the role requires. Also, how you present yourself on paper in terms of look, feel, quality and accuracy will positively impact the perception of the hiring manager.

A CV (curriculum vitae) or resume allows you to summarise your past experiences and achievements so prospective employers can get a sense of who it is they are considering for a role. It's long been part of recruitment strategies across the world. Standard CVs are likely to include:

- contact details
- a high-level statement – highlighting key job-specific attributes and career aims
- a high-level overview of key achievements and areas of expertise
- education
- previous jobs
- additional skills– such as fluency in different languages or competency with an IT package
- interests – to give a more rounded picture.

The ways in which you can share your CV

There is more work to be done beyond simply presenting a CV. A CV is not static. It has to relate to the audience that you are targeting. For example, you may choose to target specific companies and, to do this, a background search to better understand their needs will help you to tailor your CV appropriately.

Another example is that you have spoken to someone and they have asked for a copy of your CV. In this case, your CV will need to relate to the conversation that you have had with them.

However, typically, you use your CV to share with hiring agencies and employers.

Increasingly, however, if you have an online presence through LinkedIn or other social media platforms, hiring managers will check there as well, so keeping your profile in sync with your brand is imperative so that they align.

A CV *can* be useful as part of the overall picture of a candidate. Whether you have a career history detailing your experience or, if you have different or relational types of experiences to record where you have not followed a conventional route (e.g. a school leaver entering the job market; ex-military personnel; rehabilitated prisoners; returners, etc.), you can tailor your CV to align with your personal brand by skilfully tying in to reflect the relevant capabilities, potential, life experiences and passion you possess for a role.

Make sure your CV conveys your brand

If you are following a well-trodden path, your CV typically follows a logical progression through your employment history, from one employer to another, which will generally tell the story of your career to date. However, careers increasingly do not follow this path. For instance, if you have changed role or sector, your CV can start to look messy, particularly if you have done some consultancy and contractual work or have had multiple stabs at self-employment. There are also those people who return to work after maternity, a sabbatical, illness and other life events whose lives do not fit the conventional CV.

Many employers and hiring managers have specific needs which they expect candidates to fulfil – a square peg for a square hole. If you have an unusual combination of skills and experience, you are unlikely to fit a set role or profile. The odds of success are low if you are competing against candidates who do have the specific background that is being sought. However, increasingly, employers are realising that differing skills and experiences is a positive that adds value to diversity of thinking within their organisations.

It is at this juncture that doing the work of discovering who you are comes into play to show how you can add value. Having worked through the life story exercise in Part 2, it would have helped to show what worked well for you during the 'high' times and your learnings during the 'low' times. Tying all these learnings with your purpose, values and talents will enable you to truly align your CV to reflect and to demonstrate your exact offering.

That is, if you have discovered your authentic self and matched this to your needs, it will better help you to structure your CV. Not only to package your experience correctly, but also to showcase your potential, skills and passions, and evoke your archetype. In this way, you can make yourself much more attractive to an employer who wants what you have to offer and will help to cement your brand.

Tailor your CV to your market

You will use your CV in different ways, depending on who you are talking to. There are three main markets for your CV:

1 People who are introducing you

2 Prospective employers

3 Hiring managers/headhunters.

We present these one by one using an example of a standard CV for:

- a young person entering the marketplace

- an experienced hire

- a self-employed person.

People who are introducing you

A short CV can be useful for someone who may be helping you to find a job, including you in a business plan for a new venture, or inviting you to speak at a conference. Here is a format for a one-page CV that you can use in these situations:

SUNITA SHAH
*****@*****.com
Tel: +44 7*** ****89
London W1

PERSONAL STATEMENT

A young professional seeking an opportunity that enables me to widen my acquired skills and capabilities in digitisation, technology and commercial enterprise.

CAREER TO DATE

2019–present **EXTRATERRESTRIAL SOFTWARE, INC**
Apprenticeship programme rotating across key functions

EDUCATION

2014–2019 **Andrew Carnegie Primary School (Edinburgh)**
Advanced Highers: Information Technology & Economics

LANGUAGES

English: Mother tongue
Hindi: Fluent

SUPPORTING INFORMATION

As Head Girl, I developed an intranet page for the school. Its focus was to identify individual talents across the school to raise funds for a local hospice. A valuable role that has helped me to understand my leadership style as well as develop my digital skills.

I have also put together fundraising walks for charities. This supported the school curriculum in terms of us exploring different landscapes, countries and cultures such as The Highlands, Scotland and The Himalayas in Nepal.

> As goalkeeper of the school football team, I learnt the importance of teamwork and fuelled my enjoyment for collaboration. Volunteering at a local food bank has given me a deeper appreciation of inequality and poverty at all levels in our society.

Through this CV, as an apprentice, the individual is demonstrating key talents in information technology, plus leadership and collaboration while, through the extracurricular activities, she has aligned her experience with her purpose and values on issues in social justice and inequality, as well as combining her archetypes of Creator and Caregiver. She wanted to use her current skills and interests to further develop her IT capability to support her career going forward.

Prospective employers

Prospective employers often like to see a longer CV, in reverse chronological order. It's good practice to keep your CV to two pages or under. For example:

ROBERT WALLIS
*****@*****.com
+44 7*** ****65
Rochester, Kent

PERSONAL STATEMENT
To contribute to a leadership team whose focus is continued growth and digital marketing.

EMPLOYMENT

Growtomorrow PLC
eMarketing Manager – Stayfit   **2022–present**

Growtomorrow is the UK's third-largest food supplements company, with annual revenues in excess of £14m and over 15,000 employees worldwide.

Responsibilities

To develop and champion Stayfit's global digital strategy, disseminating it worldwide and to senior stakeholders. To provide company-wide thought leadership, engaging and inspiring brand teams, sharing best practice and managing an international team.

Achievements

- Led business-to-consumer (B2C) loyalty programme, based on insight and attitudinal segmentation, delivering tailored messaging during first 12 months of use, increasing loyalty in 83% of consumers.
- Developed digital strategy and launched key commercial sites to support brand positioning and communication campaigns.
- Launched a clinical trials alert service, delivering key messages to over 3000 target customers.
- Increased traffic to website by over 200%, to 80,000 visitors in 2011.
- Contributed to annual global sales growth of 47% by successfully using Display, PPC and SEO to disseminate key messages.
- Undertook competitor, situational and brand strategy analysis to run workshops and develop, agree and prioritise local digital strategy within the global strategy.
- Piloted B2C CRM strategy in two key markets to demonstrate the value of the digital channel alongside the sales force and other channels.
- Produced detailed monthly dashboards looking at key metrics and key performance indicators (KPIs) for senior stakeholders.

Newbank
Group Account Director   **2020–2021**

Responsibilities

To switch the communication strategy from a product to a customer focus, while relaunching Newbank's loyalty programme and managing the agency account team.

Achievements

- Increased warmth to bank by 25% in key segments. The softer sell was more palatable.
- Showcased bank's expertise in context, highlighting relevance where direct marketing had failed.
- Launched new, segmented magazine, increasing selling opportunities.
- Introduced robust measurement/evaluation techniques, by channel, to substantiate business claims.

Antiarms International UK
Corporate and Affinity Manager   **2018–2020**

Achievements

- New branding, new partners and products for programme, relaunched to members through major B2C campaign.
- Welcome pack and lifestyle questionnaire for new members, with response rates of 30%+.
- Data-driven promotions across a range of media, with response rates of 10% to 15%.
- Revenue increased from £100k to £330k+ per month in 24 months.
- Keynote speaker at Money Marketing conference.

Betterhealth (B2C health website)
Internet Business Development Manager   **2017**

- Developed commercial strategy for month-on-month growth of 20% through partnerships and online promotions.

➤

- Developed revenue models (market research, advertising, sponsorship) and transactional deals.
- Content syndication across various media channels.

The Major Illness Research Programme
Corporate Development Manager   **2016**

- Most successful affinity card launch: 5000 cards issued, raising over £25k in first 6 months.
- CRM promotion with Chocolight, CRC branding and royalty on 2 million containers.

Language Solutions Ltd Sales & Marketing Assistant   **2015**

- Graduate Management Training Scheme rotation.
- Part of a team administering the B2C partnership publicising Language Solutions to over 2.5 million target customers across Europe, at no cost to the company.

EDUCATION

University of Salford   **2011–2015**
BSc (Hons) 2:1 in Spanish and Economics

St Mary's College, Norwich   **2004–2011**
9 GCSEs including Maths and English
3 A-Levels – English, Spanish and Economics

ADDITIONAL INFORMATION

Nationality: British   **Languages:** Spanish and French

LinkedIn Profile: http://www.linkedin.com/name

Membership: The Rotary club

This CV demonstrates the breadth and progression of the individual's career from marketing to digitisation. His talent for strategy development, critical thinking and leadership are underscored by his values and purpose for steering innovation, in an increasingly digital world.

Hiring managers/headhunters

Recruiters often prefer a one-page summary, followed by two to three pages of detail, describing your experience. The first page can be similar to the one-page CV we showed previously. This format enables them to get most of their questions answered quickly. It also gives them the information they need to write an appraisal and present you to their clients without too much extra effort.

DAVID BROWN BSc CIPFA
Colchester, Essex
+44 7*** ***21
*****@*****.com

CAREER TO DATE

2019–present	**David Brown Ltd**
	Managing Director
2010–2019	**The Very Big Company PLC**
2014–2019	Manager, Financial Planning & Analysis
2010–2014	Financial Analyst
2006–2010	**The Big Accountancy Firm**
	Audit Trainee to Audit Manager

OTHER

2021–present	Non-Executive Director, Hi-Tech Software Plc

QUALIFICATIONS

2009	**The Institute of Chartered Accountants**
	First-time passes (Fellow 2003)
2006	**University of Manchester**
	BSc Economics, 2.1
LANGUAGES	English: mother tongue
	French: fluent business level

➤

PROFESSIONAL EXPERIENCE

2006–2010   **The Big Accountancy Firm**
2006–2009   Audit Trainee
2009–2010   Audit Manager

I joined The Big Accountancy Firm straight from university, having received offers from several of the 'Big Eight' firms. My audit clients were privately held and mid-cap companies in engineering, insurance, banking and business services.

I passed my professional examinations at the first attempt and was promoted to Audit Manager. My intention had always been to move out of the profession into industry. Within a year, I was approached to join The Very Big Company as a Financial Analyst. I accepted their offer.

2010–2019   **The Very Big Company PLC**
2010–2014   Financial Analyst
2014–2019   Manager, Financial Planning & Analysis

The Very Big Company was the global market leader in the production of High-Performance Widgets (HPWs). It had revenues of £900m and a market capitalisation of £1bn. I was based at their Birmingham headquarters, where I reported to the Deputy Group Finance Director.

I worked on many projects, including the following:

- Analysis of manufacturing costs, comparing plants in the UK, France and Taiwan. As a result, a decision was taken to close the French plant and concentrate production in the other two locations.
- Developing a financial model to evaluate a potential investment in a new production line. Using Net Present Value techniques, I concluded that the investment should proceed. The Board accepted my recommendation.

2019–Present   **DAVID BROWN LTD**

I founded my own business to provide financial consultancy to start-up ventures in the arena of sustainability. As I have developed my business offering and my team, it has afforded me the opportunity to learn about many aspects of running a business, including business development, marketing, IT and HR, and combine this knowledge with my interest in the four pillars of sustainability: human, social, economic and environmental.

PROFESSIONAL MEMBERSHIP

The Chartered Institute of Public Finance and Accountancy (CIPFA)

This CV shows that, in founding your own business, you have been prepared to step outside your comfort zone. Your talent for entrepreneurship, courage and drive is highlighted by being prepared to work outside of the security blanket of an established company. Furthermore, you are expanding your knowledge by combining it with your purpose: that businesses' ethos and practice, in the case of the example above, are to contribute towards a sustainable future.

You may find that you need to keep only two CVs updated on your computer: a two-page version and a four-page version. If someone wants a one-page CV, you can send them the one-page summary at the front of the four-page version.

Also, many hiring managers use an Applicant Tracking System (ATS). This is where your CV is scanned for key words and phrases that align with the job being advertised. It is important to tailor your CV so that this system works to help you stand out.

The importance of the covering letter

A CV sells your skills and capabilities; a covering letter presents who you are as a person and how you would add value to the role. The covering letter enables you to not only show how your skills and capabilities marry up to the role requirements, but also tells the story of how your experiences and values align with the role and the company alike. It is important that, in preparing to write your covering letter, you do research on the company that you are applying to. If you can show how the company's goals and values align with your brand, even better. The covering letter is the vehicle where you can explain yourself. This is where the archetypes and your mission can be utilised. By providing both your CV and covering letter, you are best able to capture the essence of your personal brand.

Examples of covering letters

Example 1

[Name]

[Address]

[Mobile number:] [Email address:]

Address of company applying to

Date of letter

To Whom It May Concern

Role – eMarketing Manager

I am a seasoned eMarketing professional and would like to apply for the role of eMarketing Manager at (name of company). Please see attached my CV that demonstrates a strong fit between the key requirements outlined for this role and my own experience and capabilities.

Key requirements such as:

- Deep-level expertise and a respected thought leader in digital marketing.
- Development and implementation of eMarketing strategies.
- Leadership responsibility for sizable and complex programmes.
- Proven track record of exponential sales growth.

- Excellent interpersonal and relational skills enabling collaboration with multiple and diverse stakeholder groups.

Across the years of building my eMarketing knowledge and experience, I have had the opportunity to apply commercial insight, such as my:

- Ability to see the 'big picture' through a wide-ranging perspective on business operations and practices.
- Project and resource management skills.
- Performance and results.

My way of working includes embracing challenge and forming sustained relationships with stakeholders. I am grounded in commitment and curiosity, which strongly aligns with your company values. Further, I deeply admire the cutting-edge marketing technology that your company offers and believe that being a part of an innovative team would deepen my knowledge and expertise.

I keenly await the opportunity to further discuss my experience with you and am grateful for your kind consideration.

Yours sincerely

Signature
Print name

Example 2

Dear . . .

I am applying for the role you outlined as a Development Producer of Games for your organisation.

I am very passionate about further honing my project managing skills as a producer. My strengths are being able to

➤

understand the full scope of any project and bringing on board the people I know will work well to ensure we get the project done on time and to the highest possible standard.

I thrive on making sure everyone has what they need and coordinating their talents for the best results.

For instance, in App development, it is important to me that all teams involved in its design are aligned in their understanding of the vision. My business experience and learning show that statistics and analytics from previous games/apps help to inform how to design an app.

This opportunity allows me to further enhance my skills and experience while learning from the best.

As you can see from my CV, I have recently been working on a variety of app/digital-related projects in a project manager/ producer role.

The cross-over of using both my producing and project-managing skills in those previous contracts has been really stimulating and I hope to bring my energy, skills and experience to the role you have outlined.

I look forward to hearing from you.

Kind regards

Signature

Print name

The aim is to get them to meet you

Many people think their CV and covering letter/email will get them the job they want, so they cram in too much information. Unfortunately, this greatly reduces the chances of success. The more information you give, the more information the receiver has to decide you do not fit the profile – as we have said, your CV is like a hook, you need to entice the person to want to see you – this is its primary aim . . . not to give all the information you have on yourself. The key aim is to get a meeting with the organisation you are writing to, or at least speak to someone on the phone. Your written material should give them just enough information to entice them to find out more about you.

- Your personal brand, in terms of your purpose, values, talents and skills, clearly shines through your CV/covering letter.

- If your covering letter/email is clear and concise, people are much more likely to read it. If you summarise what you have to offer in a few bullet points and, in particular, show how your values and talents align with their requirements, the recipient will be able to decide whether to read it themselves or forward it to someone more appropriate in their organisation.

- If the bullet points match some or all of their needs, they are likely to be interested in your CV. If your covering letter/email is too long or badly written, it may languish in an in-tray, until they figure out what to do with it – which often means sending you a 'thanks but no thanks' letter.

- When potential employers or business partners look at your CV, initially, they average seven seconds. If they do not immediately see how they or a colleague can use it, it is likely to end up in the 'no' pile.

- If they decide to use it themselves, they will start to spend more time on it. Be prepared for them to call you with no warning. Prepare the answers to questions they are likely to ask you.

- Avoid obvious turn-offs, such as boasting about your abilities or criticising your former employer in a covering letter. Remember that hiring managers are used to assessing the content of a CV and look for people who are realistic about their abilities.

- Be prepared to account for any periods in your CV when you have not worked. For example, you may have taken a gap year after university or a sabbatical from work to travel or study.

- Test the market by showing your covering letter/email and CV to people who have high standards and an eye for detail and are very familiar in the area. Different types of organisations have different cultures, different approaches to connecting to people and use their own 'language' . . . you do too, to get them to notice you. Get their feedback on the layout and use of English. Notice anything they find confusing and make it clearer. It is very easy to use jargon, but plain English is far more effective.

- If you have a high-quality blog or website, include the domain name prominently on your CV. That way, they can find out more about you. Videos can be very effective. Once people see you and hear you speak, they begin to feel they know you, even if they have never met you.

- Make it obvious how they should contact you. Provide one phone number and one email address at the top of your CV. (If you provide several of each, it confuses and may slow the process down.)

The clearer your communication, the more likely you are to be interviewed for roles that really interest you.

Your CV is one of several tools that people will use to find out more about you. As the world becomes more digital and increasingly visible, some companies are beginning to rely less and less on CVs and more and more on your digital footprint. For example, they may look at your personal website, including any videos that you have uploaded, as well as your Facebook, Twitter and LinkedIn pages.

LinkedIn is the digital platform for professionals and therefore the profile that companies are most likely to look at if they would like to find out more about you prior to meeting with you. With this in mind, ensure that your CV is aligned with your profile on LinkedIn and, indeed, that you regularly update it. See Chapter 14 Building your brand online, where we delve further into how you present yourself on LinkedIn.

Aligning your brand with global considerations

As globalisation becomes increasingly complex and talent becomes more diversified, it would serve you well to show how your brand proposition marries up with and takes into account issues such as diversity, equity and inclusion (DEI), environment, social and governance (ESG) complexity in terms of geopolitical and economic challenges, and the ever-present talent for the future challenges that include an aging workforce and conscious quitting.

Similarly, it would serve you well to understand how to position your brand against financial indicators and rewards. For instance, you may need to weigh up instant gratification versus long-term value. That is, at certain points, you may take on a job to fulfil practical obligations in the short term. Or you may accept a role where the pay and financial incentives are not as good as you currently have but, with the new role, you'd have an opportunity to work on an overseas assignment and thereby accrue international experience. However, ultimately, in the long term, the goal is to secure a job that is meaningful, aligns with your values, purpose and talents, and provides increased visibility and opportunities to develop, enabling you to grow as world matters shift.

Key takeaways

- Reflecting on your journey so far allows you to better understand where you are and what your CV needs to convey to get to where you want to be.

- Hooks in your CV need to refer to your experiences that you believe add value to the organisations that you are targeting.

- A CV is not static. It is an evolving document and, also, needs to relate to the audience that you are targeting, so pay attention to your hooks.

- Working through your life story will help you to better articulate your need and present your authentic self.

- Your CV must convey the personal brand that you wish to present. To be consistent, your CV should portray your purpose, values and talents.

- You can use your CV in different ways. Primarily: for people who are introducing you; prospective employers; hiring managers/ headhunters.

- Your CV presents your career and education in chronological order and it is good practice to keep your CV to two pages or under.

- Use your covering letter to show who you are as a person and how you would add value to the role. It tells a story.

- When crafting your CV and covering letter, the golden rules are: keep it simple; be clear and concise; reduce jargon and use simple English. Importantly, show how you, as a person, align with the role requirement.

chapter 16

Staying focused

The best way to market yourself is to build your personal brand. However, you have to know what you are selling. In other words, you have to know yourself. For most of us, this is a lifelong voyage of discovery.

We hope that the exercises we have offered to you in this book have helped you navigate your personal journey of discovering who you are and, in turn, strengthening your brand. If you have skipped any exercises, we strongly encourage you to go back and fill in the gaps. Discovering yourself is the most powerful way to learn; we have provided a framework to help you do so.

All the work you have done will help you to understand and better present your brand.

You will be in the best place to seek opportunities to evoke your brand. If your brand is a building, then each successful brick adds to the stability, the design and presence of your building that will gradually become distinctive.

Focusing on what you have learned about yourself gives you scope to seek different roles or business opportunities with greater clarity. If you need to change your job, you will be able to see how you can extend your brand into a related field.

It takes courage to focus on who you are. However, it is much more rewarding when you lean in and become the best person that you can be.

Knowing what you stand for makes it easier to spot opportunities that are right for you. It also helps you to ask the right questions and find out whether the culture fits your values and your way of working. The clearer you are about what you want, the more likely you are to get it. Your thoughts, feelings and actions will send out a consistent message.

Choosing roles, customers and projects

Whether you are employed or self-employed, it is worth considering the effect and impact that each new employer, customer or client will have on your brand. Salespeople are remembered for winning a particular contract that boosted their company or threatened its survival. Bankers, advertising executives, public relations consultants and headhunters are all judged by the clients they represent. Artists and musicians have contributed to many happy memories at key moments in a person's life. Successful inventors and entrepreneurs are respected for their positive legacies. If the work itself fills you with enthusiasm, you are likely to do an excellent job and strengthen your brand.

However, some people take on work they find uninspiring, feeling they have to prove themselves. Unfortunately, you are what you eat. You will become known for the work you find uninspiring and attract more of the same. You may also discourage people from giving you projects you would find more exciting.

A client of one of the authors was a human resources director who became a self-employed consultant. She planned to focus on highly paid strategic work. Then someone asked her to deal with a complicated bullying case, which she handled as a favour. This led to more of the same. As word spread that she was the expert in bullying, she attracted more of this work and less of the work she wanted to do.

Some people take on lots of projects just to keep their plates full. If you are employed, you may have to do this in order to meet your budget and keep your job. You have to decide, at some point, is it about the quantity of work or the quality? It is also important to note that, if you are kept busy doing a multitude of roles, your brand may disappear as your archetype does the same. This can lead to your expertise being diminished and, with it, your ability to increase your earnings. If the work does not fit your purpose, it can dilute your focus and weaken your brand. If you decline it, you can spend the time saved on activities that will build your brand and increase your revenues. For example, you could speak at a conference or write an article or create a podcast that potential clients will read or listen to.

Turning down work can feel like a brave thing to do. However, once you get used to doing what inspires you, you will feel more confident about it. Your state of mind is just as important as your marketing efforts in attracting the work you really want to do.

Respecting your heritage

Personal brands have a lot in common with luxury brands. In both cases, customers will pay a premium for top-quality, unique features and a distinct brand identity. There is a magic formula for luxury that can also be applied to personal brands. Successful luxury brands combine two attributes: heritage and contemporary appeal. As far as heritage is concerned, they tell you about the craftsmen who have been working away for a century or more. They also underline their contemporary appeal by employing talented designers who tap into the latest trends.

Many unsuccessful luxury brands have one attribute but not both. Some project their heritage, but the design is not contemporary. Customers dismiss these brands as *old-fashioned*. You might inherit one of their products from your grandparents, but you would not buy any of them. Other unsuccessful brands have well-known designers but discard their heritage. Their products have no consistent theme – they just follow fashion. The quality also suffers. The brand becomes *trendy* and ends up competing with other fashion items. It is unable to command a premium. Brands that have neither heritage nor contemporary appeal are *irrelevant* to consumers of luxury goods (see diagram below).

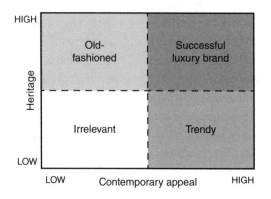

By combining heritage and contemporary appeal, successful luxury brands become far more successful and profitable than those that are old-fashioned or trendy. The same principle applies to your personal brand. Potential employers and clients are reassured by where you worked and what you did earlier in your career. It is part of your heritage. Throughout your working life, colleagues, headhunters, journalists and others will say, 'He began his career with ABC company,' or 'She practised law before starting a chain of restaurants.' Or 'They had many different jobs in call centres, creating their excellent customer service ability.' That is, your previous history provides a relevance to where you are now.

Even if you are now doing something completely different, your heritage gives people an indication of the quality of your work. It has a big impact on how they perceive you. It affects their willingness to buy from you, work with you or invest in your business.

There are two big mistakes to avoid. The first is to discard your heritage. This gives your clients less reassurance, making you less valuable to them. It is even worse to criticise your old firm, particularly if your contract was terminated and you feel sore about it. Negativity is a big turn-off and is bad for your brand.

The second mistake is to stop improving and updating your brand. After a while, you lose contemporary appeal and are regarded as old-fashioned. Saying 'When I was at IBM, we did it this way' only works for a short time. It is essential to innovate, so that what you are doing now is even better than what you did at IBM. The world moves on. You and your brand should do the same.

Continuously improving what you do

We can all improve the way we serve people. If you are committed to what you do, and excited about it, you will have the energy you need to keep learning, improving and innovating. Your work should be:

1 top-quality

2 distinctive

3 consistent with your purpose and your values

4 valuable to the people you serve.

It is important to remain conscious of how the quality of your work is presented to the world and to continuously seek to improve your brand. For instance, when you write documents, ensure that spelling and grammar are correct and that your document flows with a clear structure. That is, it has an introduction, body and conclusion. Think of your written work as an advertisement. If it is succinct and clear, it will enhance your reputation for quality.

Similarly, if you are giving a presentation, preparation is of the essence. Once you have pulled your slide pack/talk together, then rehearse. Where possible, rehearse in front of family and friends and seek their feedback. Or rehearse in front of a mirror and record yourself. This will provide you with a visual of how your body language and tone of voice come across to an audience and whether you need to modify any aspect of how you deliver a quality presentation.

In a competitive and crowded world, it is important to be distinctive. The more that you are able to set yourself apart from others, the more distinctive your brand becomes. This could include any pro bono or charitable work you do. For instance, utilising his distinctive brand, Will.i.am created the i.am Scholarship Foundation to bring educational opportunities to young people in need of financial assistance. He has also created the i.am.home Fund to help prevent struggling families in the United States from losing their homes. Will.i.am uses his celebrity platform to highlight issues and to give back to the world.

Your brand must also be consistent with your purpose and your values. Someone we know achieves outstanding Ofsted reports in the childcare sector she works in. She realised that her purpose and values correlated strongly with her love of children and, subsequently, this led her to volunteer for Great Ormond Street Children's Hospital. This adds to her brand as a Caregiver.

Finally, for your work to be valuable to your clients, it must meet their needs, some of which may be unspoken. We know a dentist who was one of the first in the UK to offer tooth whitening. He now also offers Botox, based on his knowledge of facial musculature. While few people would walk into a dental surgery looking for that treatment, many have responded to the poster in his waiting room. He knows his patients care about their appearance as well as their teeth.

If you are a specialist in one area, you can play to your strengths while seizing opportunities in other, related areas. We know a medical doctor who works as a coroner. He has also become a consultant to film directors. He helps them and their special-effects teams to ensure that every illness or injury is true to life.

Asking for feedback

The moment of truth comes when you start working on a project. Some clients and employers will give you feedback as you go along; others prefer to do so once you have finished. You may be reluctant to ask for feedback if you are afraid of criticism. However, it becomes much easier if you are committed to being excellent at what you do.

In difficult situations, feedback is important and can strengthen your relationship if your client senses your commitment. They will have even more reason to keep working with you, since you have shown you are responsive. Imagine you are a food manufacturer testing a new recipe on consumers. Some may loathe your latest concoction. Acknowledging this feedback, you might modify the recipe to take into account some of the feedback in the hope of increasing sales. But be careful not to be all things to all people. If you try to do this, then you may lose your brand in the process.

Acknowledging the fragility of brands

As we near the end of this book, it is apt to consider the fragility of individual and company brands for several reasons.

First, due to the growth of social media and its immediacy of information, it has produced the emergence of misinformation (i.e. fake news!) or immediate information. As such, it is easier for brands (e.g. companies or individuals) to be discredited or emulated. For example, during the 2020 US elections, the outgoing President questioned the accuracy of Dominion Voting Systems and its brand suffered. The accuracy of its system was eventually verified in a court case and its brand reputation restored. Similarly, the creator of the Harry Potter series, J.K. Rowling, has made controversial remarks pertaining to women, for some people, and her reputation has suffered within the transgender community.

At the opposite end of the spectrum, brands that have so far been emulated include Malala Yousafzai and Apple. Malala is a Pakistani female education activist who was shot in the head by a gunman at the tender age of 12. This terrible incident highlighted the plight of young girls who are unable to receive an education and she became the youngest winner to be awarded the 2014 Nobel Peace Prize. Emulation is also consistently bestowed on the company Apple whose innovative technology makes it the world's most valuable brand with their products becoming a status symbol across the world.

Second, a brand's reputation can shift across years. For instance, the Innocent Drinks brand was based on quality, purity of ingredients and sustainability. Following its acquisition, its brand reputation may have suffered.

Another way of shifting brand reputation is companies who would like to improve their brands. For example, cigarette companies might decide to partner with good causes in the hope that this association will improve their reputation and likewise fast food companies offering healthier food options to improve brand perception.

A combination of both brand discreditation and reputation can be seen in two examples. An advertising campaign for a well-known drink brand featured what many considered racist. The tagline was inoffensive, however, the 30-second advert was considered racist.

Similarly, fashion houses have faced brand discreditation due to their insensitive message and portrayals.

The responses on social media showed how criticism of marketing campaigns is one of the quickest ways for your brand to come under pressure.

Third, brands wanting to improve their market share can tactically pivot their brands towards trending global interests such as sustainability, the environment, and diversity, equity and inclusion. There are many examples of both companies and individuals who have done this. They believe that, by doing so, in the eyes of the customer, they are aligning their services with market forces which will increase their attraction. However, the impact is that these pivots might be perceived as 'window dressing' and not as an authentic value proposition.

Finally, it is becoming more acceptable to become a disruptive brand. A disruptive brand will undermine traditional companies in their market (e.g. Tesla, Starling Bank, Airbnb, Uber, Netflix and Amazon, etc.). The result of this is that brands have to be completely on top of their game, flexing and adapting to shifts in the market so as not to be left behind. And, while adapting, stay true to their offering.

Our point is that your brand needs to be consistent and authentic. If you decide to extend your brand into other areas that are not authentic, then this can create confusion. Strong branding is only possible if you stay true to the key elements of who you are and work to ensure these run through your brand.

Concluding remarks

Throughout this book, you have reflected on many aspects of who you are. In doing so, you appreciate that this is a lifelong journey and you are now much more focused on how you use your brand to promote yourself.

Here is a checklist to make sure you have completed the key steps to brand identification and development:

- Develop a sense of purpose.
- Identify your values.
- Identify your talents.
- Identify your unique combination of talents, skills and experiences.
- Decide which archetype (or two) you are going to evoke consistently.
- Create your hook (elevator pitch) that summarises what you do in three seconds.
- Use stories to amplify what you offer.
- Become more visible offline and online.
- Make sure your CV conveys your purpose and fits your market.
- Focus on serving people, rather than trying to get something from them.
- Proactively manage your network.
- Use social media to maintain and expand your network.
- Protect your brand and consider other ways of extending it.

- Be cognisant that your brand constantly evolves as you move through life.

If you complete each of these steps, you will build a strong memorable brand. The effects are frequently dramatic.

We look forward to hearing your story and wish you every success!

David Royston-Lee and Sylvana Storey
www.davidroystonlee.com and www.globalintegrators.org

Index